Project Management
Learn how you can take advantage today

Jonathan L. Anderson

Copyright © 2014 Jonathan L. Anderson
All rights reserved.
ISBN: 1979327009
ISBN-13: 978-1979327008

Contents

- Foreword 4
- 1 Project Management 5
- 2 Project Organizations 10
- 3 Project Estimation of Times and Cost 20
- 4 Project Plan 38
- 5 Performance Measurement 51
- 6 Risk Management 69
- 7 Docs, Audit, Termination and Closure 87
- 8 Final Remarks and further Readings 113
- 9 Endnotes 114

Foreword

Searching in any library for books on project management will definitely lead to success. Much seems to have been written about how to manage a project successfully. But why do most projects in real life still fail or end up exceeding the originally agreed upon budget, time or resources? The answer is quite easy: The project simply does not exist. Every project and as a consequence every project manager has to deal with different targets, different environments and, last but not least, with different people. Therefore, only the Know-how and the Do-how will transform a project manager into an excellent project manager.

This book is based upon the global project management experiences I gained in different positions, especially with international management consulting companies and working as a member and chairman of executive boards. I now have the pleasure to share my knowledge and gain new experiences (not only in project management) as a professor with eager and enthusiastic students.

Every project manager will develop his or her own management style in their career. Due to the constraints in the number of pages of this book I have limited the examples and case studies to an absolute minimum. Also the so-called "soft-skills" of project management could not be discussed in detail.

This book should provide the interested reader with an overview of the methods and tools which have been proven successful for project managers. Everybody who would like to have an extended reading about some chapters should refer to the endnotes, where additional references are listed.

If you have any comments, please do not hesitate to contact me at olaf_passenheim@web.de. Have fun reading the book and implementing some techniques in your next projects.

December 2017   Jonathan L. Anderson

1 Project Management

1.1 Introduction

It was just a few decades ago, in the 1950s, that modern project management was first seen as an individual subject within the area of economic sciences. Centuries back, so-called "projects" were finished successfully, e.g. the building of the aqueducts in Roman times or the construction of the Great Wall in China, but these projects were managed more on an ad-hoc basis mostly using informal techniques and tools.

Project management nowadays is regarded as a very high priority as all companies or organizations, whether small or large, are at one time or another involved in implementing new undertakings, innovations and changes etc. – projects! These projects may be individually diverse, however over time, some tools, management techniques and problem-solving approaches have proven themselves to be more rewarding than others in bringing projects to a successful end.

The development of project management has always been in parallel to the development of general trends in worldwide economics. The 1990s were all about globalization; the 2000s are about velocity and close to the edge of a new decade in which the world maybe has to face an economic recession. Nowadays, almost more than ever, everybody asks for "projects" to return the world economy to its former speed. This also underlines the importance of continuous learning and development of project management capabilities in organizations to allow corporate teams in a fast changing world to work collaboratively in defining plans and managing complex projects by synchronizing team-oriented tasks, schedules, and resource allocations.

However, gaining and sharing project information is not the only key to success. Today's information technologies allow project managers to practice and work with their teams in a real-time environment. As a consequence of this potential, project team members are able to concurrently view, act and react to the same updated information immediately.

Additionally, to external challenges, project teams are forced on a macro level to deliver satisfying results for internal or external customers and stay within the restrictions of budget, time and resources (quality and quantity). In parallel to these deliverables, executives are also asking the project management on a micro level to ensure the use of modern management tools, such as (1) customizing the project organization to fit the operational style of the project teams and respective team members, (2) informing the executive management about the project's progress on a real-time basis, (3) ensuring that critical task deadlines are met and (4) ensuring that project team members know about and monitor project risk and share accurate, meaningful and timely project documents.

As a result, the thrilling and demanding position of a project manager not only requires a particular set of skills – how to communicate, to control and to motivate people, but also the specific knowledge about tools and techniques required to run a project successfully.

1.2 Introduction

Looking at process management and project management, on one side these terms go hand-in-hand with delivering successful (project and routine) work, yet on the other side, hardly any terms more often result in confusion and misunderstandings.

According to Johansson [Johansson et al. (1993)], a process can be defined as the constitution of links between activities and the transformation that takes place within the process. This can include the upstream part of the value chain as a possible recipient of the process output. Therefore, every process has the following characteristics:

- Definability: It must have clearly defined boundaries, input and output.
- Order: It must consist of activities that are ordered according to their position in time and space.
- Customer: There must be a recipient of the process' outcome, i.e. a customer.
- Value-adding: The transformation taking place within the process must add value to the recipient, either upstream or downstream.

- Embeddedness: A process cannot exist in and of itself; it must be embedded in an organizational structure.
- Cross-functionality: A process regularly can, but not necessarily must, span several functions.

Frequently, a process owner, i.e. a person being responsible for the performance and continuous improvement of the process, is also considered as a prerequisite. The fundamental nature of a project on the other hand is that it is a temporary endeavor undertaken to create a unique product, service, or result. Projects are distinguished from operations (and therefore also from processes) and from programs.

A project will deliver business and/or technical objectives, is made up of defined processes & tasks, will run for a set period of time, has a budget and resources. Project Management deals with tracking this process' execution, from a schedule and cost perspective. It includes functions for developing the optimal project schedule, producing a financial model of the project, scheduling and tracking of effort against plan, managing costs against budget, and reporting of status, to name but a few. The uniqueness of the deliverable, whether it is a product, service, or result, requires a special approach in that there may not be a pre-existing blueprint for the project's execution and there may not be a need to repeat the project once it is completed. Uniqueness does not mean that there are not similarities to other projects, but that the scope for a particular project has deliverables that must be produced within constraints, through risks, with specific resources, at a specific place, and within a certain period; therefore, the process to produce the deliverable as well as the deliverable itself is unique.

To be temporary signifies that there is a discrete and definable commencement and conclusion; the management of a project requires tailored activities to support this characteristic and, as such, a key indicator of project success is how it performs against its schedule – that is, does is start and end on time?

Therefore, every project has the following characteristics:

- Consists of temporary activities that have predetermined start and end dates.
- Uses restricted resources.

- It has a single goal or a set of goals.
- All events are to be realized to develop a single and new output.
- Usually has a budget.
- Usually a project manager is responsible for coordinating all activities.

Projects are usually chartered and authorized external to the project organization by an enterprise, a government agency, a company, a program organization, or a portfolio organization, as a result of one or more of the following features:

- A **market demand** (e.g., a consumer product company authorizing a project to develop a new fruit drink for kids with less sugar in response to an increased health awareness)
- A **business need** (e.g., a publisher authorizing a project to write a new book to increase its revenues)
- A **customer request** (e.g., an amusement park authorizing a company to develop a new roller coaster)
- A **technological advance** (e.g., an electronics firm authorizing a new project to develop a faster, cheaper, and smaller netbook)
- A **legal requirement** (e.g., U.S. federal government authorizes a project to establish laws for controlling the home loan system)
- A **social need** (e.g., a non-governmental organization authorizing a project to raise the awareness of donating blood)

These features can also be called problems, opportunities, or business requirements. The central theme of all these features is that management must make a decision about how to respond and what projects to authorize and charter.

This book will provide a framework demonstrating how a project can be initiated, planned, executed and closed within a regular project life cycle, which also forms the conceptual framework of this book and is shown in Figure 1-1.

1.3 Conceptual Framework

Projects typically have identifiable phases and each phase has a unique set of challenges for the project manager. If we view the project from the highest level, these basic project phases can be also identified as major factors influencing the project success. If one of these phases is planned or executed wrongly, the project will have a high probability of failure.

Chapter 2 will describe the challenges of a project organization. Project management is used in almost every organization or industry; however, the bigger and therefore more complex an organization is, the more professional the approach has to be implemented for the right project organization. Specialists from different departments cannot just be pulled away from their line responsibilities or new employees can't just be hired without the internal and external communication requirements, career perspectives and the distribution of power being taken into consideration.

In **Chapter 3** the project work finally starts: The major deliverables and the participating work groups are identified. The team begins to take shape. Questions of possibility (can we do the project?) and justification (should we do the project?) are addressed.

Next is the Planning Phase (**Chapter 4**), where the project scope is further developed in as detailed a level as possible. Intermediate project outcomes and milestones are identified, along with the strategy for achieving them. Formulating this strategy begins with the definition of the required elements of work tasks and the optimum sequence for executing them. Estimations are made regarding the amount of time and money needed to perform the work and when the work is to be done.

Chapter 5 describes the execution phase: the project work is performed under the watchful eye of the project management. Performance and progress is continuously monitored and appropriate adjustments are made according to a strictly regulated change in management procedure and recorded as distinctions from the once defined strategy.
Throughout this phase, the project team concentrates on meeting the objectives regarding time, budget and resources developed and agreed upon at the beginning of the project.

Chapter 6 deals with the increasingly important requirements of risk management. Especially during the last economic crisis, it was proven that inadequate risk management systems played an important role more in many project disasters. Proper risk management tracks the progress of outstanding action plans, describes who is responsible for those actions, and sets the expected timeframe for resolution.

As shown in fig. 1-1, the arrow points again to chapter 3, defining the project scope. This, however, just reflects the idea and practical experience that rarely does a project comes within the set boundaries of time, budget or resources. Project Management also has a lot to do with constantly rehearsing and slightly adapting the original project scope in a controlled way.

2 Project Organizations

2.1 Conceptual Framework

The ambition is to achieve technologically and economically the best results in the development of continuously more complex and organizational problem-solving strategies. Complex tasks in large organizations require the greatest possible co-operation between corporate divisions and specialists and requires a great deal of multidisciplinary. The more project work becomes important for affected organizations, the less traditional management and organizational concepts will be successful. Traditional organizations are mainly characterized by a split-up between competence and management (leadership), which is focused on an efficient and effective job processing. Project management seems the ideal solution to maximize the possibility of the successful completion of a task, which is, by definition, time-limited.

But the implementation of project teams within the organizations can not only be challenging, but also dangerous, as the fulfilment of a project task has usually never been achieved before and therefore implies a lot of uncertainty, especially for the project member affected. Looking at the institutional side of project management – mainly structural aspects of the organization, the link with the parent organizations as well as Human Resources are considered. Questions concerning the best project organization, the (personnel) configuration of the project team and the decision powers also have to be answered. As a project is mainly run under time restrictions and therefore tolerance for adaption or failure-correction is hardly available, the set-up of the project organization is probably the largest obstacle to project success.

When deciding on a project organization it should be the aim to give the involved departments and project members a maximum degree of freedom in their decisions, to consider personnel restrictions and requirements of the organization and to avoid havoc caused by unclear job descriptions or an accumulation of co-ordination requirements.
But also, simply choosing the best position of a project organization – between a pure line organization and a pure project organization, won't necessarily be successful. By using such a standardized roadmap, opportunities and risks of different organizational structures cannot be seen and "power centers" and areas of conflict cannot be identified.

The common understanding of project managers nowadays is that there is not a single best option for setting up a project organization. The chosen organizational structure has to reflect the requirements of the project and the organizations, has to fit the possible requirements as well as technological opportunities of the future and therefore is the best balance between technological and human-social factors. Project Management has to identify prior to a project start the internal and external requirements in order to give the best possible recommendation for a successful project.

2.2 Project Organization and Responsibilities

The structural organization is a static framework of an organization that defines on one side the internal distribution of tasks to individuals or departments, and on the other side the relationship between the individuals/departments. While the structural organization defines who has to do a job, the operational structure follows a more dynamic approach, namely when, where and how often something has to be done.

In Project Management, the structural organization has to fulfil two tasks:

- Definition, how a project organization is embedded within the parent organization (organizational models, see discussion below).
- Definition, how the organization is structured internally within the project team.

The **project sponsor** is the manager or executive within an organization who is not directly involved in the operational work of the project but who can oversee a project, delegate authority to the Project Manager and can provide support as a trainer or coach to the Project Manager.
The Project Sponsor has sufficient authority or influence to direct all the staff involved in a project – or as many as possible – and to get the co-operation of key stakeholders. He ensures that the project is aligned with the organizational strategy and compliant with policy. In larger projects, he has frequent contact with the Project Manager so as to monitor his effectiveness. Depending on the initial set-up of the project he can also chair the Steering Committee, approve final deliverables and communicate about the project inside the agency and with external stakeholders.

The **steering committee** is a group of senior managers responsible for business issues affecting the project. They usually have budget approval authority, make decisions about changes in goals and scope and are the highest authority to resolve issues or disputes. The steering committee assists with resolving strategic level issues and risks, can approve or reject changes to the project with a high impact on timelines and budget and has to assess project progress and report on the project to senior management and higher authorities. The steering committee provides advice and guidance on business issues facing the project and they use influence and authority to assist the project in achieving its outcomes.

Both the project sponsor and the steering committee also have to carry out the **project governance** of a project. As much as corporate governance is required nowadays not only in stock listed companies, project organizations also require compliance with certain rules. Governance in general can be described as all activities and processes which ensure that directors and managers act in the interests of the organization and are accountable for their use of those assets.

Project governance is carried out by regular review of project documents, such as plans and status reports, looking for evidence that the project is in the interests of the organization and uses assets responsibly. In discussions and decisions, the person responsible for the Project Governance has to vote for what he believes is best for the organization and its stakeholders. To fulfill all these requirements, it is compulsory that the Project Manager and his team demonstrate competence, ethics, and compliance with organizational policy.

An **advisory committee** is a group of people that represents key project stakeholders and provides advice to the project. Like steering committees, advisory committees are generally recruited from senior management. Unlike steering committees, advisory committees cannot make decisions regarding a project. Their role is to provide insights to the team regarding stakeholder interests, technical advice and other relevant initiatives. Parallel to the steering committee, they assist with resolving issues and risks and should use their influence and authority to assist the project in achieving its outcomes and to communicate about the project progress within their organizations.

The **project manager** is naturally the key person within the project organization and has the overall responsibility for meeting project requirements within the agreed to time, cost, scope and quality constraints which form the framework of the project plan. Project managers report to the steering committee, which has delegated its authority to the project manager. The general tasks of a project manager are:

- Supervision and guidance to the project team
- Regular (weekly or monthly) project status reports to the project sponsor/steering committee
- Chair risk and change control committees (if applicable for a project)

- Attend steering committee meetings and prepare supporting materials with the project sponsor
- Execute project management processes: risk, issues, change, quality, and document management
- Ensure project plan, schedule and budget are up-to-date; detect and manage variances

A **team leader** is a person responsible for managing one part of a project, or a "subproject." This position only exists on larger projects where subprojects are required due to the number of employees involved or different project goals allow the parallel work. A team leader ideally has project management skills, including human resource management, in addition to relevant technical skills. Usually, junior project managers are selected for this position. A team leader reviews all sub-team deliverables, holds regular sub-team status meetings and provides regular status reports to the project manager.

Last but not least, a **team member** is a person assigned to a team who is responsible for performing a clearly defined part of the project activities. Depending on the organizational set-up a team member may report directly or indirectly to the project manager and is assigned to work part-time or full-time on the project.

2.3 Organizational Models

There are two fundamentally different ways of organizing projects within the parent organization:

- The project as part of the functional organization or pure line organization
- The project as a free-standing part of the parent organization (project organization)
- A third type, called a matrix organization, is a hybrid of the two main types

The **pure line organization** or **functional organization** (see Figure 2-2) does not have a specific position for project managers. Project managers are specialist or line managers who are aligned to the project for a specific time. The project is divided into partial tasks and delegated to responsible departments. The team members continue to report to their line-directors and upper managers.

The advantages are:

- Reduced overhead, as no additional project team members have to be hired
- Provides clearly marked career paths for hiring and promotion
- Employees work alongside colleagues who share similar interests, therefore the expertise of the team members stays within their departments
- No structural change for running the project required
- Flexibility for changes in the project scope
- Easy post-project transition as the project team members simply continue doing their line job again

The disadvantages are:

- Co-ordination of functional tasks is difficult as little reward for co-operation with other departments is granted since authority resides with functional supervisor
- Provides scope for different department heads to pass off company project failures as being due to the failures of other departments
- Slow reaction time due to long communication lines within the project

Within the **pure project organization** ("task-force") the project manager is fully responsible for a group of specialists, which have temporarily dedicated their entire workforce to the project.

The advantages are:

- Simple and fast, as the project manager has full line authority over the project and all members of the project team are reporting directly to the project manager
- The lines of communication are shortened; the ability to make a swift decision is enhanced

- A cross-functional integration is supported as a pure project organization can maintain a permanent cadre of experts who develop skills in specific technologies
- A project team that has a strong and separate identity and develops a high level of commitment from its members
- The organizational structure tends to support a holistic approach to the project

The disadvantages are:

- Each project has to be fully staffed which can lead to a duplication of staff numbers
- Project managers tend to stockpile equipment and technical assistance as this represents the importance of their project within the organization
- Pure project groups seem to foster inconsistency in the way in which policies and procedures are carried out
- In a pure project organization, the project takes on a life of its own, with own rules and processes
- The post-project transition is difficult as there tends to be concern among team members about career after the project ends

The matrix organization as shown in figure 2-4 is a combination of a functional and a pure project organization. This organizational structure allows for participation on multiple projects while performing normal functional duties. A greater integration of expertise and project requirements can be achieved.

A matrix organization can take on a wide variety of specific forms:

"**Project**" or "**strong**" **matrix organizations** most closely resemble the pure project organization. The project manager decides work- and personnel-progress, the line manager provides resources and consults the project manager as a specialist.

The "**co-ordination**" or "**functional**" or "**weak**" matrix most closely resembles the functional form. The project manager only co-ordinates the contributions of the different departments, the authority stays with the department-directors.

The "**balanced**" **matrix** lies in between the others. Project and line managers approximately have equal competence and agree upon a common decision.

The advantages are:

- The advantages of a functional organization and project team structure are retained
- Resources can be coordinated in a way that applies them effectively to different projects
- Team Members can maintain contact with project teams as well as with their functional department colleagues, they can be chosen in-time, according to the needs of the project
- The project team will be more agile and able to view problems in a different way as specialists have been brought together in a new environment.
- Project managers are directly responsible for completing the project by a specific deadline and budget.
- Team members can return to their old line responsibility after finishing the project

The disadvantages are:

- Potential for conflict between functional vs. project groups due to unclear responsibilities as the principle of unity of command is violated with a matrix organization
- A conflict of loyalty between line managers and project managers over the allocation of resources
- Costs can be increased if more (project) managers are created through the use of project teams
- The balance of power between the project and functional areas is very delicate
- The division of authority and responsibility in a matrix organization is complex and uncomfortable for the project manager
- Project workers have at least two bosses, their functional heads and the project manager.

2.4 Choosing the Project Organization

Choosing the right project organization is the first and probably the most important key to success for project management. Therefore, a great deal of time should be spent in considering the decision about formation, preparation and initiation of the project organization.

Best practice is a step-wise approach, to define the goals and implications of the project within the current organizational structure:

Step 1: Definition of the project, with a statement that reflects the major outcomes from all different points of view (top management, shareholder, stakeholder etc.). Standardized decision matrixes are available in a wide range with experienced project managers. However, the following points already will give an indication of what should be considered:

- Size of project
- Strategic importance, how important is the project to the firm's success?
- Novelty and need for innovation
- Integration requirements (departments involved)
- Complexity (number of external interfaces)
- Budget and time constraints
- What level of resources (human and physical) is available?
- Stability of resource requirements

Step 2: Determination of the key tasks which are linked with every sub-goal or objective and identification of the specialist/individuals within the parent organization and their "home" departments.

Step 3: Breaking down the project into tasks and determining which organizational units are required to carry out the work packages and which units will work particularly closely with which others (this will be discussed in more detail in the next chapter).

Step 4: List of any special characteristic or hampering factor associated with the project.

Step 5: With the findings gained from steps 1- 4 and the knowledge of all advantages and disadvantages choice of structural organization form.

Recent developments are showing that companies tend more and more to change the project organization during the project.

The advantages of different project organizations are utilized by such an approach. During the planning period, maximum knowledge of different departments can be given to the project, while not all team members have to be involved full-time in the project. In the realization phase, a pure project organization helps the project team to solely concentrate on the fulfilment of the project goals and in the last stage, team members can more easily reintegrate into their line function by selecting a functional project organization and can help to integrate the newly found knowledge into their "**home**" departments.

The organizational set-up determines the way a project is delivered. An effective organization is therefore crucial to the successful delivery of projects on time, to budget and to specification. Therefore, a great deal of time and attention should be given to project organizations when initiating new projects.

Effective project organizations have to identify all key positions across the wider organization, also including the advisory team, the steering committee and the sponsor, if possible. After deciding upon these key roles, clear terms of reference and accountabilities for all key roles and bodies; e.g. project manager; steering committee have to be set up and also communicated (in writing) to the project team. The position and the role of the organization framework, like supplier, partner or customer interfaces has to be defined at all levels, along with their specific responsibilities towards the project.

The operational structure also has to include the ways of working for the team, detailing how the work with key partners, supplier and the customer will be executed and, last but not least, a governance structure for the project has to be developed.

2.5 Conclusion

The project organization is one of the first "visible" parts when a new project is started. Many industries are beginning to realize the benefits of closer working relationships and more integrated working environments on projects.

Approaches like collaborations and co-operations have existed for some time, but many organizations resisted, often on the grounds of cost, to adopt such methods.

Project Management is starting to mature at individual and corporate levels, and businesses are understanding not just the benefit, but the fundamental need to adopt such practices if they are going to deliver projects 'faster, better, cheaper'. Such aims are truly attainable, but only if less effective organizational practices are replaced by more concurrent and integrated project organization during key phases of projects.

In some cases, this involves businesses working together much earlier in the project cycle, which can challenge traditional methods and thinking. Many industries are now realizing that the benefits far outweigh the risks, and are embracing new "**ways of organization**".

3 Project Estimation of Times and Cost

3.1 Introduction

This chapter will provide a framework as to how to define the project scope and how to estimate times and costs. Project Management is usually always about meeting the issues in the magic triangle: scope, time and cost. If one of the goals is missed or wrongly planned, the project's success usually can only be achieved by reallocation of more resources, which costs money and/or will take more time. Planning is the key to careful overview and balances these three parallel goals. Top-down and Bottom-up approaches can be used. This chapter illustrates which tools exist to identify activities and how to sequence and schedule them in a positive way and how a bridge between these steps can be built. Last but not least methods for estimating the time, the progress and the cost for projects are shown.

3.2 Project Kick-Off Meeting

Experienced project managers know that it is crucial to get projects off to a successful start. According to one veteran project manager: "The first team meeting sets the tone for how the team will work together. If it is disorganized, or becomes bogged down with little sense of closure, then this can often become a self-fulfilling prophecy for subsequent group work. On the other hand, if it is crisply run, focusing on real issues and concerns in an honest and straightforward manner, members come away excited about being part of the project team." [Gray/Larson 2002].

Holding a good kick-off meeting is an efficient way to commence. A kick-off meeting is a meeting held at the beginning of a project but not until the first tasks of the initial phase are completed. The project charter is already set up and the project team is aware of the peculiarities of several stakeholders. There are three typical objectives project managers try to achieve during the first meeting of the project team.
The first is to provide an overview of the project, including the scope and objectives, the general schedule, methods and procedures. It is important to establish basic rules as guidelines for the upcoming work. The second is to begin to address some of the interpersonal concerns captured in the team development model:

- Who are the other team members?
- How will I fit in?
- Will I be able to work with these people?

The third and most important objective is to begin to model how the team is going to work together to complete the project. The project manager will recognize and evaluate for the first time the behavior of the team members. This can be critical, especially in intercultural teams where often different kinds of behaviors and personalities can be observed, which can have a high potential to collide.

3.3 Project Scope Management

Defining the project scope sets the stage for developing a project plan. Project scope is a precise explanation of the expected result of the project or product for the customer from an external as well as from an internal point of view in a specific, tangible, and measurable way. The scope should be developed under the joint direction of the project manager and customer. The project manager is responsible for an agreement with the customer on project objectives, deliverables at each stage of the project, technical requirements, etc. The project scope will be fixed in a document. Depending on its complexity it is stated in the project charter if it is at a manageable level, or in a special project scope statement frequently done on large projects. These documents are normally published and used by the customer and the other project participants for planning and measuring project success. Scope describes what one expects to deliver to the customer when the project is complete. Due to the high priority of the project scope, a checklist including all elements of the project plan is a favorable way to ensure that scope definition is complete. A project scope should contain the following elements:

1. Project objective
2. Deliverables
3. Milestones
4. Technical requirements
5. Limits and exclusions
6. Reviews with customer

Project objectives and deliverables already have been discussed several times in this book. A **milestone** is a special event in a project that is reached at a point in time. The milestone schedule shows only major segments of work. It represents first, rough cut estimates of time, cost and resources for the project. The milestone schedule is built using the deliverables, as a platform to identify major segments of work and an end-date. The **technical requirements** have to ensure the proper performance. For example, a technical requirement for a project with a university library could be that a student can be identified with his Computer IP-Address if he logs in into an internal database, to enable the university to track down any misuse. The importance of technical requirements is obvious because such a malfunction on a project could cause enormous damage. The **limits and exclusions** should be well defined. Failure can lead to false expectations and to expending resources and time on the wrong problem. The completion of the scope checklist ends with a **review with the customer**, internal or external. The objective is the common understanding and agreement of expectations. Is the customer getting what he or she desires in deliverables? Does the project definition identify key accomplishments, budgets, timing, and performance requirements? Are questions of limits and exclusions covered? Clear communication on all these issues is imperative to avoid claims or misunderstandings.

Many projects suffer from scope creep, which is the tendency for the project scope to expand over time, usually by changing requirements, specifications, and priorities. Scope creep can be reduced by carefully writing the project charter or project scope statement. A scope that is too broad is an invitation for scope creep. Scope creep can have a positive or negative effect on the project, but in most cases scope creep means added costs and possible project delays. Changes in requirements, specifications and priorities often result in cost overruns and delays. Examples are abundant: The Trans rapid train project in Shanghai, the opening of the new terminal at Heathrow Airport, etc.

Setting clear project priorities, listed depending on their importance, also helps to avoid a scope creep. The management and/or the costumer define the order of priorities in accordance with their needs. Therefore, the priorities can be set arbitrarily and vary from project to project. The three important factors for the success of a project are the meeting or exceeding of the expectations of the costumer and/or the management in terms of costs (budget), time (schedule) and performance (scope). The interrelationships among these criteria vary and can be seen as trade-offs between the project team and the customer.

The trade-offs among time, costs and performance have to be allocated and managed by project managers. The trade-offs in a project occur between scope, cost and time. It should make clear that project managers have to balance these three points (regarding the magic triangle). If one of these objectives is missed, a project easily fails. In order to evaluate priorities there has to be a candid discussion between project managers, customers and upper management to establish the relative importance of each criterion. The work breakdown structure and the priority-matrix are tools which are used in practice to identify and define which criterion is constrained, which should be enhanced and which can be accepted.

The **Work Breakdown Structure (WBS)** is a grouping of the work involved in a project oriented towards the deliverables that defines the total scope of the project. The WBS can be imagined as a roadmap of the project which breaks down the total work required for the project into separate tasks and helps group them into a logical hierarchy (see example fig. 3-2). Different levels of detail assure the project managers that all products and work tasks are identified in order to integrate the project with the current organization and to establish a basis for control. Furthermore, the WBS organizes and divides the work into logical parts based on how the work will be performed. This is important as usually a lot of people are involved in a project and many different deliverables are set to reach one main objective to fulfill the project.

In addition, to this, the WBS serves as a framework for tracking cost and work performance because every element which is defined and described in it can be estimated with reference to its costs and time needed. Consequently, the WBS enables the project managers to make a solid estimation of costs, time, and technical performance at all levels in the organization through all phases of the project life-cycle.

Decomposition is the key to success in creating a professional WBS. Decomposition describes the process of subdividing project deliverables into smaller, more compact and manageable components until the work and deliverables are defined at the work package level. This aforesaid work package is the lowest level in the WBS, and is the base at which the cost and schedule for the work can be estimated in a reliable way. The complexity of the project determines the level of detail for work packages.

To follow a hierarchical breakdown, it is reasonable to start with the project as the final deliverable. Afterwards, the different deliverables can be decomposed into work packages. The decomposition to a lower level of detail enhances the ability to plan, manage and control the work. On the other hand, project managers have to be careful with the decomposition of sub-deliverables because an exaggerated decomposition can lead to non-productive management effort, inefficient use of resources, and decreased efficiency in performing the work. Therefore, the project team has to find the balance of the level of detail during the planning process.

Outputs after creating a WBS are in most cases an update of the project scope statement and a draft of **Project Communication Plan (PCP)**. Change requests as a result of the created WBS can be accepted. Afterwards the project scope statement is updated to include those approved changes. The key document generated by the WBS process is the actual WBS. Each WBS component is generally assigned a unique identifier from the code of accounts. These provide a structure for the hierarchical summation of costs, schedule and resource information.

When the project deliverables and work packages are clearly identified it is essential to communicate them to all project members in the right way.

Poor communication is a major contributor to project failure in most cases. Communication is a key component in coordinating and tracking project schedules, issues, and action times. The PCP is a fundamental part of the overall project plan because it maps out the flow of information to all different stakeholders in a project. When developing a PCP, the following points should be considered:

- Stakeholder communications requirements
- Information to be communicated, including format, content, and level of detail
- Identification of who will receive the information and who will produce it
- Suggested methods or guidelines for conveying the information
- Escalation procedures for resolving issues
- Revision procedures for updating the communications management plans
- A glossary of common terminology used on the project

To develop a PCP which considers these points one has to follow these basic steps:

Stakeholder analysis: Identifies the target groups. Typical groups could be the customer, sponsor, project team, project office, or anyone who needs project information in order to make decisions and/or contribute to the project processes.

Information needs: What information is important for whom? For example, top management needs to know how the project is progressing, whether it is encountering critical problems and the extent to which project goals are being realized. This information is required so that they can make strategic decisions and manage the portfolio of projects. Furthermore, team members need to see schedules, task lists and specifications, so that they know what needs to be done next. External groups need to know changes in the schedule as well and they need to know performance requirements of the components they are providing.

Sources of information: When the information needs are identified, the next step is to determine the sources of information. Information can be collected using milestone reports, team meetings, and project status meetings.

Distribution modes: One of the most common distribution channels in modern companies is e-mailing. There are of course other methods through which information can be distributed, for example through teleconferencing, Lotus Notes, SharePoint, SAP and a variety of database sharing programs. Companies can use the "Web" to create "virtual" project offices in which to store project information. Project management software is used by companies to transfer information directly to the Web site so that different people have an immediate access to relevant project information. In some cases, it is a standardized routine that important information is transferred directly to key stakeholders.

Responsibility and timing: Determine who will send out the information. For example, a common practice is to have minutes of meetings or specific information forwarded to the appropriate stakeholders. Other centers of competence can be the project manager or the project office. Timing and frequency of allocation appropriate to the information needs to be established.

One advantage of developing a PCP is that the flow of information is controlled by a certain person or department which is responsible for it. Furthermore, it is not necessary to respond to information requests because everyone who is involved in a project is supplied with the requisite information.

3.4 Activity Resource Estimating

Activity resource estimating (ARE) is closely related and coordinated with the cost estimating process. The schedule for activity resource estimating involves determining what resources (staff, equipment, or material) and in what quantity each resource is needed.

Inputs for the estimation are in general:

Enterprise Environmental Factors: The infrastructure resource availability information can also be found in the project charter. These factors can be, for example, the organizational or industry standard, the existing human resource or the personnel evaluation system.
Activity List: The activity list identifies the schedule activities for resources that are estimated.

Activity Attributes: The activity attributes provide the primary data input for use in estimating those resources required for each schedule in the activity list.

Resource availability: Information on which resources are potentially available is used for estimating the resource types. This knowledge includes consideration of various geographical locations from which the resources originate and when they may be available.

Major tools and techniques for such an are:

- An expert judgment which is used to rehearse the resource-related inputs. Any group or person with specialized knowledge in resource planning and estimating can provide such expertise
- An alternatives analysis which includes such thoughts as, for instance, make or buys, hand versus automated, different size or type of machine
- Published estimating data which are routinely published by various companies, e.g.
- on production rates and unit costs of resources for an extensive array of labor trades, equipment for different countries and geographical locations within countries
- PM-Software, that helps planning, organizing, and managing resource pools and develops resource estimates
- Bottom-up estimation which is used when a scheduled activity cannot be estimated with a reasonable degree of confidence, whereby the work within the scheduled activity is decomposed in more detail.

The **output of the activity resource estimating** process is an identification and description of the types and quantities of resources required for each scheduled activity in a work package.

Resources Breakdown Structure: The resource breakdown structure is a hierarchical structure of the identified resources by resource category and resource type.

Resource Calendar: A composite resource calendar for the project documents working days and non- working days that determine those dates on which a specific resource, whether a person or equipment, can be active or is idle. The resource calendar typically identifies resource-specific holidays and resource availability periods.

Request Changes: The activity resource estimating process can result in request changes to add or delete planned scheduled activities within the activity list.

3.5 Project Time Management

The **project time management** includes the necessary processes to finish the project on time. All of these processes interact with each other and with processes in the other organizational competence. Each process can involve effort from one or more persons or groups of persons, based on the needs of the project. Each process occurs at least once in every project and occurs in one or more project phases, if the project is divided into phases. Although the processes are described as individual items with clearly defined interfaces, in practice they may overlap each other and correlate in interactions.

On some projects, especially ones of a smaller scope, activity sequencing, activity duration estimating, and schedule development are so tightly linked that they are viewed as a single process that can be performed by a person over a relatively short period of time. These processes are presented here as distinct processes because the tools and techniques for each are different.

Activity Definition

The essential basis of project time management is the definition of operations. The activity definition is essential and used consistently as the basis for all further steps in project time management. The definition of operations includes the determination and documentation of their respective operations, therefore transactions are structured and defined in individual work packages/tasks. Each operation identifies a fixed deferred activity. The execution requires time and effort.

The operations must be accomplished to the work breakdown structure so that the specified and partial delivery items can be developed. This process imperatively implies the need for defining the processes so that the project objectives can be achieved. The work breakdown structure (WBS) is the essential tool with which to describe the activities in detail.

Activity Schedule

The determination of an operation sequence enfolds the determination and the documentation of the relationships between the operations. The process flow must exactly be defined, so that a realistic and practicable time plan can be put into action later. That may be determined manually or with the help of special computer software. If few details are known, manual processes are often better suited for smaller projects and in the early stages of larger projects. Manual and automatic procedures can also be used in combination.

Inputs are the activity list as a tabulation of activities to be included on a project schedule and the product description which includes product characteristics that often can affect activity sequencing, such as a physical layout of a plant to be constructed or subsystem interfaces on a software project.

The process of **estimating schedule activity durations** uses information on schedule activity scope of work, required resource types, estimated resource quantities and resource calendars with resource availabilities. The input for the estimates of schedule activity duration originate from the person or group on the project team who is most familiar with the nature of the work content in the specific schedule activity. The duration estimating is progressively elaborated upon, and the process considers the quality and availability of the input data. The activity duration estimating process requires that the amount of work effort required, the assumed amount of resources to be applied to complete the schedule activity is estimated and the number of work periods needed to complete the schedule activity is determined. All data and assumptions that support duration estimating are documented for each activity duration estimating.

The **schedule development** is the instruction regarding the start and finish date for a project activity.

If the start and the finish dates are not realizable, the project will probably not be finished on time. The time schedule development process must be often repeated before the project time schedule will be finished.

Schedule control is concerned with (a) influencing the factors that create schedule changes, determining the current status of the project schedule, (b) determining that the project schedule has changed, and
(c) managing the actual changes as they occur. Schedule control must basically be connected with the other control procedures.

3.6 Estimation of Project Cost

An important part of project management is the project cost management. It covers the scopes of cost estimations and budgeting. Moreover, cost control ensures that the project stays within the financial borders which are defined in the budgeting process.

Although the estimation, budgeting and control of costs are defined as three unaffiliated processes   in theory, they are strongly related and interacting. Significant for the project cost management is its concentration on the cost generated by the performance of the project schedule. But in addition to this, it should also deal with the effects of the cost management decisions on the project deliverable, in the form of 'life-cycle costing'. For example, saving costs in research and development in the construction phase could decrease the quality of the final goods and therefore put the project's objectives at a risk.

At this point it has to be mentioned that in most industrial applications of project management, for example the industrial manufacturing of products, the financial performance of the project's deliverable itself is not taken into detailed consideration. The responsibilities for these calculations are distributed outside the project. In contrast, in projects in the financial sectors the analyzing and forecasting of the product is a fixed task of the project cost management. So one can see that the way the project cost management is dealt with varies according to the different requirements of each project.

Also, the ways and points of time measuring of the project costs have to be adapted to the project's character and also to the special needs of the individual stakeholders. This means, in detail, that a rough cost estimate has to be done before the management can give its blessing to the project. In the next step, the project managers should make a new, more detailed estimate, which should be reported to all project stakeholders, especially the project sponsor, and more than ever in the case of a deviation from the first rough estimate. In this case the budget or the project's scope or aims have to be changed. Such a control of estimates should be done continuously by gathering more and more details.

The stakeholders also will be interested in the basis values on which the assumption was made. These should be documented in a detailed way as a foundation for recalculations and to ensure the ability to find potential fault. Because of the traditional high value of labor costs, this calculation should be well structured and cover all needs of direct and indirect labor.

The overall estimate of all costs should be allocated to the single project tasks, so that the individual manager's performance can be measured on this 'baseline'.

In order to estimate the project cost and to generate an appropriate budget, it is necessary to have an overview of the different kinds of costs that are implemented in the nature of projects. One can define three main types of costs, which are the direct costs, e.g. costs for direct labor or material, the direct overheads, which are already a bit harder to grasp, and last, the general and administrative overhead costs. The direct costs are the most important costs in project cost management. Because of their close link to individuals they are easy to influence. This can be an advantage in project planning or in budget problems, but, and this is the key factor, they have to be paid close to the date of progress too. A closer look at the organizational resources that are used in project performance is given through the direct overhead costs. These are all those costs which can be linked to the product, but are not directly countable and must not directly be paid. But of course the project cost management has to bear them in mind in the long run, to ensure profit and staying within budget.

They are allocated to the project costs by the direct cost driver. Furthermore, an organization which executes a project also has overhead costs that cannot be linked directly to the project, obviously, although those costs, for example costs for maintenance, senior managers' salary or accounting, have to be covered by the projects during the time of project performance. According to the direct overhead costs, the general and administrative overhead costs are allocated by the cost driver of the direct costs.

The project cost management's task in cost estimating is to examine the different possibilities to spend costs in various project steps, with the aim of ascertaining which opportunity generates the greatest savings. So it may be that the project team is able to save some costs in production or execution, for example through higher productivity or improvements in product development, by spending a larger amount of money in the engineering phase. Furthermore, the steady improvement of the project cost estimate's accuracy is another challenge the project cost management team has to meet. This is done by continuously refining the calculated values, by taking more and more details into consideration which are discovered during the performance of the project. A typical experience in the field is the desire to have a 90 to 95 percent probability of meeting time and cost estimates. The remaining planning gap will occur due to unforeseeable challenges like change requests etc.

Inputs for the estimation of the costs of a single activity from the project's schedule are the amounts of all resources which are required to perform that activity. If the performing organization does not provide these skills, they have to be supplied by the project management team.

Another document which provides necessary information to facilitate the creation of the cost estimate is the Work Breakdown Structure. It describes all tasks that are included in the project's progresses and their relationship. One can find a detailed description of these tasks and of all requirements of the project's deliverables in the work breakdown structure. A general overview about the execution, monitoring and controlling of the project is provided by the project management plan.

Many inputs are required to create a comprehensive project cost plan:

Firstly, the environmental factors have to be stated. These are for example the marketplace conditions. The market place conditions include available products and services on the market and by whom they are supplied. Internal or commercial databases can be used to obtain general information about material and equipment prices or other resource cost information.

The second important factor is the consideration of well-known data and predetermined approaches. These are often prearranged policies in organizations, which define the operation boundaries and templates which were developed to guide the project management team's performance of necessary tasks. Information collected from prior projects is often a great help in estimating the resources the actual project will need. This information could consist of documents, records or simply the experience the team has had in earlier projects. Nevertheless, the project cost managers have to bear in mind the project's uniqueness in environment and application, and that therefore the complete acquisition and utilization of these historical data will not necessarily lead to a result. Those unique factors are stated in the project scope statement, for example, special contracts, legal implications, technical issues or constraints in delivery times, available resources or cost limits of a project.

The third and most important part of the project cost plan is the schedule management plan. This document, containing the activity resource estimating and the activity duration estimating, lists all activities that are necessary to complete the project, their durations and resources requirements. This is the basis upon which to calculate the project's direct costs. Depending on the duration of the project, the expenses for financing and interest rates will vary and with increasing duration the accuracy of the estimates will decrease.

Last but not least, the project team itself has a great influence on the project's performance quality and the accuracy of the estimation. The more experience the team has in executing projects and the better they work together as a team, the less time, and therefore costs, will be required for the planning phase.

Furthermore, people who concentrate only on one project at a time will do their work more effectively than people who have to split their attention between various projects. Also, the individual personal skills of the team members will have great influence on the reliability of their estimations.

Many managers responsible for certain tasks in the project's progress tend to extend their estimations for a certain percentage, to ensure that they will stay within budget or will even be under budget. This behavior is called "padding". So the project cost management should know about these inclinations and handle them by negotiations or by shortening the budgets.

An often used time, cost and resource estimate method, especially in software-engineering projects, is the so called 'function point method'. It uses weighted variables, called function points, for the main requirements, for example inputs, outputs or interfaces. Every single item of these items is multiplied with a complexity factor that gives a value to the complexity of performing or programming the item. The factors are defined on the basis of the information collected from prior comparable projects. The total sum of the functions points multiplied by the complexity factors describes the workload of the project.

Now, the amount of function points that one person can discharge in one month is set as "one person- month".

With a fixed number of persons working on the project, the project manager can calculate how many months will be the project's duration and therefore, by multiplying the number of months by the workers' salaries, the estimated labor costs. Of course this approach works the other way around to. If the project duration is set, one is able to calculate how many staff members are needed to perform the project.

The estimate's accuracy of course depends on the reliability and the comparability of the historical data the estimate is based upon.

All these top-down estimates have one weak point in common: They have only scant regard to the detailed work structures, base their estimates on experience and give little due to very specific individualities in comparison with prior or standard projects.

Therefore, it is advisable to use the top-down estimating only for rough estimates in the initial phase of a project. To generate more detailed and accurate estimates, the bottom-up methods are used in later phases of the project, when more specified information is available.

Although the bottom-up estimations can claim to be very accurate in meeting the project's requirements, experience tells us that the actual total cost tends to exceed the estimations.

Therefore, many companies multiply the estimations by a security factor around 120 percent.

The reasons for this inaccuracy can be traced to the estimation process itself (maybe the top manager pushed the estimates down) and the changeable predictability of the future.

The factor that causes the greatest differences between estimation and reality is that the estimates of the tasks are mostly done independently from other tasks. But of course all tasks belonging to the project's performance are linked and therefore dependent on each other. The time and costs that are necessary to co-ordinate the interactions of the individual progresses increase exponentially the more people and the more tasks are integrated into the project, but even so they are often not taken into consideration.

Furthermore, are the estimations based on normal conditions? It is assumed that everything runs the way it should run. The problem is, mostly normal conditions are not the case in reality. Bottlenecks in material supply or restructures in human resources or simply failures in performance will crop up and affect the time and cost schedule. These situations can be taken into consideration in creating the cost estimations as "known unknowns", but their extent and their effects are still unquantifiable.

3.7 Conclusion

It takes more than just being a good manager to deal with the environment and all other important issues which may come along with a project in the initiation and planning process.

Through sufficient attention, emphasis on involved people, tailored tools and techniques and experience gained from prior projects, one transforms him or herself into a good project manager. Of course this can be a learning process which takes a whole working career.

At the beginning there is the complex process of identifying and prioritizing the people who are involved in or affected by the project. This is the first benchmark for the project manager. One has to see the project from different points of view to get an idea of what the expectations and desires of particular stakeholders could be. A mutual exchange of these expectations and sufficiently tailored communication channels are required to set the basis of success. Additional formal documents concerning the project are an advantage and are a necessity so that stakeholders are able to revert to stated facts should some issues become unclear. One can see that a combination of conservative approaches like formal issues to set the framework and creative and open-minded approaches to manage the stakeholders is compulsory to finish an initiation process which is the key for a successful start to the planning process.

The planning process comprises issues like project scope, work break-down structure, and estimation methods for time and cost as main topics. So, as one can see, there is a wide range of steps involved in planning a project. For such a large number of tasks at a high level of complexity it is important to use a guideline. Tailored approaches for each task and company will function best but often there is a lack of resources for such a perfect approach. The estimation methods are divided into two major approaches, the top-down and the bottom-up approach. Often the question arises whether, in the general view, the top-down is the best approach or exactly the other way around. Probably both approaches are the correct. At the beginning of a project it is favorable to set a framework and create the big picture using the top- down approach. Later, short and quick decisions based on expertise are required and here a bottom-up approach is more suitable.

What the author wants the reader to realize is that current and future project managers should expend major efforts in listening to people who are in the project environment and try to retain the big picture of a project.

4 Project Plan

4.1 Introduction

Project working is the fulfilment of a task under the constants of time pressure, so time is an extremely important measurement for project efficiency. Because of all these challenges in executing projects it is important to have a project plan. A project plan provides a great deal of information for every stakeholder whose work is related to the project. A project plan in the beginning is a simple planning tool, however while working on the project it will become one of the most important control instruments and after ending the project it is a measurement of whether the project has reached its goal. This chapter will explain how to develop a project plan, about the terminology in project plans and what different approaches to project plans are used in practice. The different approaches to project networks will be explained: **Pert, Critical Path Method, Activity on Arrow, Activity on Node Network** and **Gantt Charts**. These different methods and approaches have been chosen because they all are used in projects, and many firms have defined one method as a standard within their firm.

4.2 Developing a Project Network Plan

A project network is the basis for scheduling budget, equipment, labor, communications, the estimated time consumption and the start and the finish dates. To structure a project network and define a standard which many people are able to use, the following terminology was defined for use in project networks. Figure 4-1 shows an example of a project network plan.

An **activity** is an element of the project network; activities are tasks which are defined to complete and to meet the goals of the project. An activity needs time to be completed. It has resources like personnel, budget, space and, in most instances, relationships. An activity in a project network shows which tasks have to be performed in order to proceed, which resources are needed and how many of them. As the name implies, a **parallel activity** is a task which is processed at the same time, parallel to other tasks.

When using parallel activities, the consumption of resources will rise because they are required at the same time.

A **merge activity** is one activity which follows on more tasks; parallel activities come together in this activity. A succeeding activity can only be started when all preceding processes are ready.

An **event** is something which doesn't consume project time; an event is generally a date. To define the start date or a date when something is delivered is an event. An event can also be the kick-off or the ending and many dates between.

A **path** is the connection between the depending activities. It has no duration and is the visualizing of the relationship between the activities. The critical path is the shortest duration of the project. It is on this path that the most activities without buffer are placed and it is extremely important to know at which point on the critical path the project is because if an activity on the critical path is delayed, that delay will alter the total project duration.

The **critical path** is probably the most important outcome after drawing a project network plan. Every project has such a path and the workflow of all critical tasks sum up to the critical (shortest) duration time. All other tasks which are not on the critical path do not have an impact on the project. They could cause a delay which will have no impact on the finish, or in other words: that delay would be highly unlikely to be so long as to affect the critical path. With the knowledge about the critical path the project team can act and react.

The following basic rules should be applied when developing a project network plan:

Networks flow typically from left to right. That is a must because only a common approach ensures that the project team knows how to read the network, developed out of the Western writing logic. An activity can only be used once: it is not allowed to make loops, where an activity has to be fulfilled several times. If the same task has to be repeated, a new activity has to be drawn up. An activity cannot begin until all preceding connected activities have been completed.

This is rather logical as it is not possible to begin something until the preceding tasks have been completed. This fact has to be shown in the network.

Arrows on networks indicate precedence and flow; they can cross. To show the flow of the process and to show which tasks have to be done, arrows are used.

Each activity has to have a unique identification number: numbers help to support orientation in the network. The number of the activity shows the workflow. With numbering of activities it is easy to follow the path through a project. Normally the numbering of activities should be done in an ascending order, that means the start activity should have the lowest number and the last activity should have the highest number. Each activity needs a unique identification code; most computer programs accept numeric and alphabetic codes or a combination of the two. The planner or project manager should leave gaps between numbers (5, 10, 15, ...), so he can add activities later. This is necessary because it's nearly impossible to draw a perfect project network from the beginning. Most times activities are forgotten or activities must be divided into smaller pieces. We showed that situation in the example above.

Clear tasks have to be used to show the beginning and the ending of the project. The project network is a plan which has to support the workflow in the project. Everybody has to know what his part and task in the project is. To show the beginning date is extremely important because it shows the project team members that they have to meet the goal of the project with the beginning of a new activity. It is also extremely important to define the end date. The defining of the beginning and ending tasks has to do with the controlling of the project and the definition of dates, which have to meet while the project is proceeding.

Milestones are activities which have a special task in the project. They are control points of the work which is done up that date. The milestones give the project team members and especially the project manager the ability to measure the workflow of the project while working on it.

This has the advantage that they can control the project while working on it, thus enabling them to react when something goes wrong and to do something in the preceding project time so as to still be able to meet the goal of the project without missing the final day. Milestones are the important control tool in using project networks.

"If-than-else" (conditional) statements are not to be used in project networks. This rule is rather a psychological rule; conditional statements can reflect possible insecurity and the reader of the project network may get the feeling that the task is not manageable. To show that the project is well organized and will be successful it is important to use sentences which show that the activity will be successful.

The work breakdown structure is the first step in setting up a project network. The second step is to enhance the activities with information. The resources necessary to complete an activity are the most important: needs of labor, equipment, time, costs, space etc. It is also important to ascertain what the relationships and the dependencies of the activities are. The third step in developing the project plan comes with the implementation of the information into the project network plan.

4.3 Activity-On-Node Network Techniques

Easy to handle software with a good graphical output and the rising availability of personal computers increased the work with so-called activity-on-node (AON) network plans. The following figures and explanations outline the basic principles used for designing an AON network:

An activity is represented by a node which can take different forms but is normally represented as a rectangular box. The activities are connected by arrows between these boxes. The arrows represent the dependencies between the different activities and the specific sequence in which the estimated tasks must be accomplished. The length and the slope of these arrows do not provide any information about operational hours, workload etc., they just improve the readability of AON-plans by improving the visual clarity of the dependencies between the activities of a project.

To establish activities into a project the project manager and its team have to define the relationships of each activity in the project context. This can be done by answering the following three questions for each single task:

- Which activities must be finished before starting this one?
- Which activities can directly start after finishing this one?
- Which activities can be done in parallel to this one?

After answering these questions, the project team knows the so-called predecessor, successor and parallel relationships for each task that has to be done. Gathering this information is essential for the development of a graphic flow chart for the project activities in order to make all these dependencies between the different activities visible.

Figure 4-2 shows a standard network plan. All tasks are successively done and the project manager knows that activity B cannot start until A is done, and that activity C has to wait for task B. In this case task A is the predecessor activity for task B and activity A and B are the predecessor tasks for activity C.

Figure 4-3 shows that the activities Y and Z have to wait until the task X is ready. In this case activity Y and activity Z can be done in parallel. The graphic shows that it is possible to run these two activities at the same time in order to save time, for example. The final decision as to how to organize these tasks is made by the project manager. Sometimes the availability of resources leads a project manager to organize activities in a row instead of using the chance of working in parallel.

A project manager who organizes the activities for house building, for example, has often to deal with limitations on the availability of construction workers. He has to decide whether e.g. the foundation for the house or the garage is done first, although these tasks could be done at the same time.

The number of arrows running out of a node in an AON-Plan indicates how many activities are immediately following. The activity X in figure 4-3 is called burst activity because more than one arrow bursts from its node.

Figure 4-4 shows another possible situation in an AON-network. Task J, K and L can be done in parallel if enough resources are available and no other constraints are existing. Activity M has to wait for task J, K and L to be done until it can be started. For example, a roofer cannot start his work for a house until the foundations and the walls are ready.

In this case, activity M is called a merge activity because more than one task must be completed before it can start. In figure 4-5 activities X and Y can be done in parallel. Also, task Z and task A can take place at the same time but have to wait until the predecessor activities X and Y have been done.

Knowing this basic information, it is important to follow the next example in developing an AON- network. It is also important to remember the essential rules named before.

Arrows can cross over each other like in figure 4-4; the lengths of the arrows make no statement about task duration. It is important to create a logical and accurate inclusion of all project activities including all their dependencies and time estimations. Table 4-1 contains information about simplified activities that have to be done to install a new suspension bridge.

The first steps in building an AON network based on the information given in Table 4-1 are shown in figure 4-6. Task A is the first node that is drawn, because it has no preceding activity. Activities B, C, D, E and F are directly dependent upon task A. The project team members have to wait until they obtain approval for building such a suspension bridge before they start the installation of the foundation and fabrication of all units needed. Each of the preceding activities is connected by an arrow with task A, because the remaining succeeding activities can be done at the same time when task A is "ready". Figure 4-6 shows the complete network of our example project. The project manager can find all activities and their dependencies in graphical way.

4.4 Time Calculations

Developing an AON-network is the first step in calculating the start and finish times of the activities.

The times estimated for each activity need a realistic base to create a reliable AON network.

The times estimated for the suspension bridge example (Table 4-1) are simplified and provide only the basis for explaining the rules for calculations in AON-networks. A project manager only needs to make some easy to handle computations to create the so-called **forward pass** – earliest times and **backward pass** – latest times.

The **forward pass** questions to be answered are:

I. How soon can the activity be started? (Early Start – ES)
II. How soon can the activity be finished? (Early Finish – EF)
III. How soon can the project be finished? (Expected Time – ET)

The **backward pass** questions to be answered are:

I. How late can the activity be started? (late start – LS)
II. How late can the activity be finished? (late finish – LF)
III. Which activities represent the critical path (CP)? (This is the longest path in the network which, when delayed, will delay the project.)
IV. How long can the activity be delayed? (slack or float – SL)

4.4.1 Forward Pass – Earliest Times

The forward pass starts with the first project activity and detects each path (chain of sequential activities) through the network until the last project activity is reached. As the path is traced the activity times are added. The longest path denotes the project completion time for the plan and is called the critical path.

Table 4-2 provides information about the duration of each activity that has to be done to complete the wind energy plant example project.

Figure 4-7 shows an enhanced node layout where additional information can be stored.

For the suspension bridge example, the times for each activity are taken from the list as shown in table 4-2 and were put into the field "duration" for each activity. For example, activity A has a duration time of 5 days and activity H of 10 days.

To start with the forward pass computation a start time has to be defined. In this case the start time is 0. In "real life" developing a project network is certainly dependent upon calendar dates with weekends and holiday etc. The suspension bridge example is simplified to support the placement of the principles of AON- networks.

The early start (ES) for the first activity, A, is zero. This time is found in the upper left corner of the activity A-node in figure 4-7. The early finish (EF) for activity A is 5, because (ES + Duration = EF; 0 + 5 = 5). Activity A is the predecessor to activities B, C, D, E, F. The earliest start date for these activities is 5, because all of them are directly following on from activity A and hence they have to wait until activity A is finished. To compute the early finish (EF) for activity B, C, D, E and F the formula ES + Duration = EF is used.

- EF(B) = 5 + 10 = 15
- EF(C) = 5 + 10 = 15
- EF(D) = 5 + 20 = 25
- EF(E) = 5 + 15 = 20
- EF(F) = 5 + 10 = 15

Now it is important to choose the right earliest start for activity G, because activities C, D, E and F are preceding this activity. There are three possible answers but only one is correct. The calculations of the early finish of activity C, D, E and F produced three different results: 15, 20 and 25. Because all activities immediately preceding activity G must be completed before G can begin, the only possible choice is 25 days. Because activity D will take longest to complete, it controls the early start of activity

G. Now activities B and G are preceding the next, activity H. Looking to the largest early finish of both leads to the right solution for the early start date of activity H. As calculated before, the early finish of B is 15 and the early finish of G is 30, so the early start of activity H is 30. The next activity I has only one preceding activity. After calculating the early finish of H by using following formula: ES + Duration = EF (30 + 10 = 40) it can be carried to I, where it becomes its early start. The same procedure is used to compute the early start for the last activity J. So the EF of activity I (40 + 5 = 45) becomes the early start of I. Now the early finish of J (45 + 5 = 50) shows the earliest possible time the whole project can be completed under normal conditions.

Rules for forward pass computation:

I. Activity times along each path in the network (ES + Duration = EF) are added
II. The early finish (EF) is carried to the next activity where it becomes its early start (ES), unless
III. The next succeeding activity is a merge activity. In this case the largest early finish number (EF) of all its immediate predecessor activities is selected

After the forward pass computation, the graph for the suspension bridge example will look like in fig. 4-8:

4.4.2 Backwards Pass — Latest Times

The backward pass calculation starts with the last project activity on the network. Each path is traced backwards and activity times are subtracted to find the (LS) and finish times (LF) for each activity. Before the backward pass can be computed, the late finish for the last project activity must be selected. In early planning stages, this time is usually set equal to the early finish (EF) of the last project activity (or in the case of multiple finish activities, the activity with the largest EF). In some cases, an imposed project duration deadline exists, and this date will be used. In the suspension bridge example, the 50 days of early finish of the whole project are accepted also as the latest finish of the project and hence the EF of activity J is carried to its LF. To compute the backward pass only three rules, analog to the forward pass, are needed.

I. Activity times are subtracted along each path starting with the project end activity (LF – Duration = LS)
II. The LS is carried to the next preceding activity to establish its LF, unless
III. The next preceding activity is a burst activity; in case you select the smallest LS of all its immediate successor activities to establish its LF

These rules are used to compute the backward pass of the wind energy example. First the LF of activity J (50 workdays as mentioned above) is subtracted with its duration (LF – Duration = LS; 50 – 5 = 45). The thereby calculated LS of J is directly carried to activity I where it becomes its LF. The LS of activity I (45 – 5 = 40) is again directly transferred to activity H (LF). The LS of activity H (40 – 10 = 30) may directly affect the two activities G and B. In the case of activity G, it is clear that the LS of activity H is directly transferred to the LF of G, because activity H is its only immediate following activity. The LF of activity B is controlled by the LS of activity H. The latest activity B can be finish is 30 days. The LFs of activities C, D, E and F are only depending on activity G so their LF becomes 25. The LS dates of activities B, C, D, E and F which are all affecting the LF of the first activity A are computed below.

- LS(B) = 20 – 10 = 20
- LS(C) = 25 – 10 = 15
- LS(D) = 25 – 20 = 5
- LS(E) = 25 – 15 = 10
- LS(F) = 25 – 10 = 15

As with the rules detailed above, the smallest LS of activity B, C, D, E, and F is the right choice for the LF of activity A, in this case the LS of D, because activity D takes the longest time to complete in this comparison. The LS of activity A (5 – 5 = 0) completes this backward pass, all latest activity times are known.

Figure 4-9 shows the totally filled in graph after the calculations are made:

4.4.3 Identification of Slack or Float

When the forward and backward passes have been computed, it is possible to determine which activities can be delayed by computing "slack" or "float". Total slack or float for an activity is simply the difference between the LS and ES (LS − ES = SL) or between LF and EF (LF − EF = SL). Figure 2-11 shows different examples, slack for activity B is 15 days, for activity E 5 days and for I 0 days. The slack gives information about the amount of time an activity can be delayed without delaying the whole project. If slack of one activity in a path is used, the ES for all activities that follow in the chain will be delayed and their slack reduced. Use of total slack must be coordinated with all participants in the activities that follow the chain. After slack for each activity is computed, the critical path(s) is (are) easily identified. When the LF = EF for the end project activity, the critical path can be identified as those activities that have LF = EF or a slack of zero (LF − EF=0 or LS − ES = 0). The critical path in the suspension bridge example is represented by activities A, D, G, H, I and J (Figure 4-10). A delay in one or more of these activities would delay the whole project.

A network schedule that has only one critical path and non-critical activities and that enjoys significant slack would be labeled insensitive. Conversely, a sensitive network would be one or more critical paths and/or non-critical activities with very little slack. Under these circumstances the original critical path is much more likely to change once work gets under way on the project.

AON-networks have different advantages. For example, they are easy to draw and the logical structure and the simple elements used help the project manager to design such networks. Another advantage is that indirectly involved persons, like first-level managers, are able to understand the main points and problems of a project quite quickly by using an AON-Network because the graphical representation helps to bring everything that influences the project into well-arranged context.

The computations needed to develop an AON-Network are quite simple and easy to handle. On the other hand, an AON-Network without a graphical printout is virtually useless, because only a table including all facts and figures with a graphical representation can be read efficiently? AON-Networks created with modern computer software can help the project manager to arrange his daily work in an efficient way and to concentrate on other important tasks.

4.4.4 Scheduling Techniques

Network scheduling techniques form the basis for all planning and predicting and help management decide how best to use its resources to achieve time and cost goals. Managers can cope with the complexities, masses of data and tight deadlines that are characteristic of highly competitive industries by using these techniques. They make all steps of a project more transparent, so it's easier to recognize dependencies between activities, to schedule risks, to identify critical paths and to evaluate how delays will influence project completion. There are several different scheduling techniques, but the most common ones are network diagrams like the AON method and the Program Evaluation and Review Technique (PERT).1

The Program Evaluation and Review Technique is a network analysis technique which uses the AOA or AON approach to estimate project duration. PERT has the ability to deal with uncertainty in activity completion times. It can help to develop more realistic schedules to reduce cost and time requirements. This is a great advantage compared to the critical path method. The CPM is more deterministic and uses fixed time estimates for each activity. Time variations, that can have a great impact on the completion time of a complex project, will not be considered. For the performing of PERT estimates, a three-point estimate for each activity is required. A three-point estimate is an activity duration estimate that includes an optimistic, most likely and pessimistic estimate. The optimistic estimate is based on a best-case scenario. Generally, it is the shortest time in which the activity can be completed. The most likely estimate is based on an expected scenario. The completion time has the highest probability. The pessimistic estimate is based on a worst-case scenario. That is the longest time that an activity might require.

Often, only a discrete estimate, for example the most likely estimate, is used to estimate activity durations. If now the PERT should be used to determine a project schedule, numbers for the optimistic, most likely and pessimistic duration estimates for each project activity have to be collected. For example, the duration of two days is estimated for an activity, it would be the most likely time. Now, an optimistic time has to be estimated. In this case it could be one day and the pessimistic estimate could be nine days. Without using PERT, the duration will be fixed at two days. After collecting the numbers, the PERT weighted average can be calculated:

With this example, the difference between PERT and the critical path will be clarified. The duration of the activity is fixed at two days with the critical path method. But with the PERT method the duration of three days is determined. This is a good example to show that PERT has the ability to deal with uncertainty in activity completion times.

The main advantage of PERT is that it attempts to address the risk associated with duration estimates. The disadvantages of this method are that several duration estimates are required and the method is not the best one for assessing risks.

4.5 Conclusion

The project plan is the "visualization" of the work breakdown structures. All information gathered so far is combined and links and dependencies between individual tasks are visible. Project times can be tracked and, most important, critical activities in terms of times and resources can be planned, rehearsed and optimized. The critical path is the most important outcome of a project plan. It is important to understand the critical path to know where you have critical activities and where you do not. There might be a lot of activities that end up running late, but the overall project will still complete on time since the late activities are off the critical path.

5 Performance Measurement

5.1 Introduction

Evaluation and control are part of every project manager's job. This part keeps the whole project on-track, on time and within budget. Depending on the size of the project, control will be either simple or complex. Sometimes it is absolutely enough to control the project by "wandering around" and/or "involvement" to overcome most problems in small projects. But large projects need some form of formal control.

Control holds people accountable and prevents small problems from becoming big ones. Each project should be assessed for the appropriate level of control needed: too much control is too time consuming, too little control is very risky. For effective control, in the best case the project manager needs a single information system to collect data and report progress There are three major points which have to be covered to build up the framework for a functioning project control system:

- What data to collect; how, when and who will collect them?
- Analysis of the data and
- The report of the current status.

Before starting any control system, one should think of the metrics which will be used for project control. If time is a key performance indicator, more data will be required than for a performance measurement on budget. Typical key data collected are actual activity duration times, resource usage and rates, and actual costs, which are compared against planned times, resources, and budgets.

After the project manager has determined which data have to be collected, it is time to establish how, when, and who will assemble the data. Is the project team, the contractor or even the project manager himself responsible for this job? Sometimes even independent cost engineers are hired for this job. In the case of data such as cash flow, machine hours, labor hours, or materials in place, it can be collected electronically.

How long is the reporting period? Again, this question has to be answered individually for every single project. Sometimes one week is enough but there are other projects where the manager needs to know the actual status on a daily basis. As explained before, it is important to provide the right information to the right people. Data which is important for the project manager could be useless for a stakeholder. Senior management's major interest is usually: "Are we on time and within budget? If not, what corrective action is taking place?"

5.2   The Project Control Process

To set up an effective and efficient project control structure only a few basic steps are required:

- Setting a baseline plan
- Measuring progress and performance
- Comparing plan against actual
- Corrective action

The **baseline plan** provides the elements for measuring performance. It is derived from the cost and durations information found in the work breakdown structure database and time-sequence data from the network and resource scheduling decisions. From the WBS the project resource schedule is used to time-phase all work, resources, and budgets into a baseline plan.

Basically there are two forms of **measuring progress and performance**. The relatively easy and obvious way is the quantitative measurement of time and budget. These figures can be implemented easily into the integrated information system. Parallel one has to observe the qualitative measures such as meeting customer technical specifications and product function. They are most frequently determined by on-site inspections or actual use.

In practice it is easily said easily that a project will be finished early, on time or late. Measuring performance against budget (e.g. money, units in place, labor hours) is more difficult and is not simply a case of comparing actual versus budget.

The probable biggest problem with plans is: They seldom materialize as expected. Therefore, it is crucial to **compare a plan against actual**, measured deviations and to determine if action is necessary. Periodic monitoring and measuring of the status of the project allows for comparisons of actual versus expected plans. While the project's problems are small, and detected early, it is possible to solve them with a minimum of effort. This is why the timing of the status reports is very important. Usually status reports should take place in a period when proactive correction is still possible.

If the comparison between plan and actual results includes significant deviations, **corrective action** will be needed to bring the project back in line with the original or revised plan. In some cases, conditions or scope can change which, in turn, will require a change in the baseline plan to recognize new information.

Monitoring Time Performance

A major goal of progress reporting is to catch any negative variances from plan as early as possible to determine if corrective action is necessary. Monitoring schedule performance is relatively easy. The project network schedule, derived from the WBS, serves as the baseline to compare with actual performance.

Gantt charts (bar charts) like those used in modern project management software and control charts are the typical tools used for communicating project schedule status. The Gantt chart is the most favored, used and understood. This kind of chart is commonly referred to as a tracking Gantt chart. Gantt and control charts serve well as a method for tracking and trending schedule performance. Their easy-to- understand visual formats make them the favored tools for communicating project schedule status – especially to top management, who do not usually have time for details. Adding actual and revised time estimates to the Gant chart gives a quick overview of project status on the report date.

Figure 5-1 presents a baseline Gantt chart and a tracking Gantt chart for a project. The solid bar below the original schedule bar represents the actual start and finish times for completed activities or any portion of any activity completed.

A **control chart** is another tool used to monitor past project schedule performance and current performance and to estimate future schedule trends. The chart is used to plot the difference between the scheduled times on the critical path at the report date with the actual point on the critical path. Control charts are also frequently used to monitor progress toward milestones.

As a result of the performance tracking either via a Gantt chart or a control chart, a progress report has to be written and distributed. Before doing so, one has to consider that a progress has primary and secondary audiences.

Primary audience is your client and all of the people working directly on the project, including other information developers, subject matter experts, marketing planners, production assistants, and the information development manager. These people will closely read the report and check for information that directly affects them, such as an issue that you assign to one of the recipients to solve.

The secondary audience are all the other people with an interest in the project, but no hands-on responsibility, including the managers of subject matter experts, marketing staff other than marketing planners, trainers, and executives who are responsible for ensuring that the communication product is available. These people will skim the report to make sure that the project is progressing smoothly and note any issues that might affect their work.

The progress/status report should not extend beyond one page if a project manager wants people to read the report. The use of charts and headings is highly recommended so that recipients can easily scan the report to find just the information they need. The following information should be included:

- Milestones: If a milestone was scheduled during the time period covered by the report, it has to be mentioned whether or not it was achieved. If yes, mention if the project is on or ahead of schedule. If not made, it has to be explained why it was missed and when it is expected to be made.

- Budget: Indicate whether the budget is exceeded or not. The indication of the percentage of the total budget that has actually been spent gives an idea about the anticipated total cost by this point in the project.
- Changes which were made, for what reason and authorized by whom.
- Quality which is met by e.g. the guidelines "editorial, production, and usability".
- Challenges (Technical or Project Oriented): Issues have to be prioritized by their affect towards the project goal and information has to be provided:
- Who is responsible for resolving the problem?
- Date by when the person responsible must resolve the problem.
- Current status (completed, in-progress, action delayed).

Even with the above described approach it is not always easy to keep control of a project. It is easy to detect large changes in scope. The biggest danger of scope creep exists when there are many "minor refinements" that eventually build to be major scope changes that can cause problems. Although scope changes are usually viewed negatively, there are situations when scope changes result in positive rewards. Scope changes can represent significant opportunities. In product development environments, adding a small feature to a product can result in a huge competitive advantage. A small change in the production process may get the product to market one month early or reduce product cost. During a product life cycle, changes are unpredictable and will occur. Some changes can be very beneficial to project outcomes; changes having a negative impact are the ones we wish to avoid. Careful project definition can minimize the need for changes. The price for poor project definition can be changes that result in cost overruns, late schedules, low morale, and loss of control. Change comes from external sources or from within. Externally, for example, the customer may request changes that were not included in the original scope statement and that will require significant changes to the project and thus to the baseline. Internally, stakeholders may identify unforeseen problems or improvements that change the scope of the project.

Data acquisition is time consuming and costly. People who have certain responsibilities in the field of monitoring and control need additional time for these tasks. In some cases, data exist but are not sent to the stakeholders who need information relating to project progress. Clearly, if the information does not reach the right people in a timely manner, you can expect serious problems. Your communication plan developed in the project planning stage can greatly mitigate this problem by mapping out the flow of information and keeping stakeholders informed on all aspects of project progress and issues.

With your information system in place, you need to use your communication plan to keep stakeholders informed so that timely decisions can be made to ensure the project is managed effectively.

5.3 Performance Indicators

Performance indicators help an organization to define and measure progress towards organizational goals, especially toward difficult to quantify knowledge-based processes. Performance indicators are measurements that reflect the critical success factors of an organization which are agreed up front. Different kinds of organizations vary in their indicators. For example, a company has a performance indicator as the annual sales volume, while a school may focus its performance indicators on graduation rates of its students. The selected performance indicator should reflect the organization's goals and is typically tied to an organization's strategy. They should be measurable and chosen in long-term considerations on stable values.

Performance indicators related to projects are measures of project impacts, outcomes, outputs, and inputs that are monitored during project implementation to assess progress toward project objectives. Later they can be used to determine whether the project was successful or not. These indicators organize the information in a way that clarifies the relationships between the project's impacts, outcomes, outputs, and inputs and helps to detect problems during the project which could delay the project finish date.

Often the risks and factors which have a high influence on the project were poorly identified and the chosen objectives have no standardization across units – since it depends on the judgement of individuals to define them. At the same time the ratings can be too optimistic.

Without appropriate feedback regarding the project development, no participant (stakeholder) can make suitable decisions about whether and how to adjust the project's layout to achieve a project's intended objectives.

Performance monitoring can be profitable when the tool is used correctly. Periodical measuring of a project's progress toward explicit short- and long-term objectives and giving feedback on the results to decision makers who can use the information in various ways to improve performance is the correct way to use this method. The correct application of performance indicators provides a project manager with a high-level, real-time view of the progress of the project. They may consist of any combination of reports, spreadsheets and charts. They may be sales figures, trends over time or any long-term considerations which are essential for the project. It is important that the indicators are measurable and accurately defined. For example, if an organization sets the goal to be the most popular company, this value cannot be measured, calculated or compared to others, therefore this performance indicator would be useless.

The needed information and data collection efforts become evident as project objectives are formulated. In a performance monitoring system, indicators serve as tools for measuring the flow of change. Baselines are the values of performance indicators at the beginning of the planning period; targets are the values at the end.

The benefits of indicators come from their measurability and from their direct source from project objectives, which are grounded in sector, economic, risk, and beneficiary analysis.

Indicators specifically link the project's inputs and activities with quantified measures of expected outputs and impact.

Before selecting indicators, one must consider which measures of performance will tell them whether and how a project's proposed objectives are being achieved and decide what project managers should do in response to the indicator outcomes.

5.3.1 Indicators

It is necessary for a project manager or organization to identify the performance indicators in advance. At the same time performance indicators must be based on the unique objectives of individual projects. The approach of the World Bank for example gives a clear and understandable overview of the project. It is a planning tool and is best used to help project designers and stakeholders when thinking about the framework of their project.

- Set proper objectives
- Define indicators of success
- Identify activity clusters (project components)
- Define critical assumptions on which the project is based
- Identify means of verifying project accomplishments
- Define resources required for implementation

This framework can improve the identification, preparation, and performance evaluation process, making it transparent to project members and providing a logical approach in designing the project.

The framework assumes that projects are mechanisms of change and that they are selected from among alternatives as the most cost-effective way of achieving a desired outcome. That brings together several project management perspectives such as results-oriented management, basic scientific method and cause and effect. For these management perspectives it is helpful to use performance indicators to measure progress with certain objectives.

The following examples indicate different ways to measure the performance of a project:

Result indicators measure results relative to the project objectives and should be defined prior to the start of the project.

Input indicators measure the quantity (sometimes quality) of the resources concerning the project activity such as funding, human resources, equipment and material.

Output indicators measure the quantity (sometimes quality) of the goods or services created. Depending on the project it can be – miles of road built (a street project), patients vaccinated (by a public health project).

Outcome and impact indicators measure quantity and quality of the results achieved through the provision of project goods and services such as increased vehicle use or traffic counts (through road construction or improvement), reduced incidence of disease (through vaccinations).

Relevance indicators: some projects have intended impacts on national goals or even unintended negative impacts which can be measured with evaluations studies. Relevance indicators measure trends in a broader perspective e.g.: reduced transportation costs (through road construction or improvement), and improved national health as measured by health indicators (through improved health care, health system performance).

Risk indicators measure the status of factors identified as critical for example factors that are determined to have a direct influence on the outcome of various aspects of the project (such as, economic prices for power or competitive salaries for project staff). These external factors should be favorable to the project.

Efficiency indicators represent the ratio of inputs needed per unit of output product, for example dollars, physical input or labor required per unit of outputs.

Effectiveness indicators represent the ratio of outputs (or resources used to produce the outputs) per unit of project outcome or impact. For example, miles of road build per unit increase the vehicle usage, or new road usage per unit decrease in traffic overcrowding. Or number of vaccinations administered per unit decline in morbidity rate or per unit decline in mortality rate.

Sustainability indicators represent the long-term benefits of a project, particularly after the project ends.

For example, maintenance and use of roads after highway construction ends or disease rate trends after external funding for a vaccination project ends.

5.3.2 Measuring performance

The above listed indicators are measured by impact, outcome, input, output, and risk indicators and can be expressed and gathered in different ways. The choice of indicators depends on time constraints, data availability and cost-benefit consideration as well as the relationships between the indicators.

Direct measure relates to any performance level, for instance quantities of goods delivered or number of clients served are direct measures of output.

Indirect measure is less precise than direct measure. They are often used when direct measures are too difficult, costly or inconvenient to obtain. Indirect measures are based on a known relationship between the performance variable and the measure chosen to express. For example, number of passengers in public buses as an indirect measure of decreasing traffic holdups.

Performance indicators should be meaningful and relevant to the project, a reliable system for collecting data must be developed, as well as the capacity and willingness to monitor and evaluate the information.

The routine monitoring and evaluation of the project sometimes does not provide sufficient information. In this case additional in-depth analysis with special studies can help to solve unexpected problems.

5.4 Monitoring, Evaluation and Control

It is essential to identify the concept of monitoring, evaluation and control to focus the elaboration especially on these key figures. Monitoring is the umbrella term for all kinds of instant systematic capture, observation and supervision. The function of monitoring is to intervene for corrective action in observed operations and processes if these do not develop as planned.

Thus, monitoring relating to a project is to identify drawbacks and intervene for corrective action.

Generally, evaluation means the description, analysis and estimation of projects, processes and organization units. Evaluation can relate to the general framework, structure, process as well as the result (product). Evaluation in terms of project management is then its estimate with reference to required value. Besides planning, organizing, staffing and directing, control is an important managerial function. It helps to check the errors and to take corrective action. Modern concepts identify control as a foreseeing action whereas in former days' control was to correct detected errors. In fact, control means to detect and rectify errors and prevent reoccurrence.

In conclusion, these three terms have their own meaning if they stand alone. Nevertheless, it works as a system if they coexist. Figure 5-2 shows the interdependence of the three terms. Thus, monitoring leads to evaluating and evaluating to control.

In different approaches, not all of these aspects occur. They are based on only two of these aspects: monitoring and controlling. This is a result of the short distance between evaluating and monitoring, respectively evaluating and controlling.

Schwalbe [Schwalbe 2007] describes a very sophisticated control system which is based on the ideas of Duncan [Duncan 1996], which is also used very often in practice and is based on inputs, tools, techniques and outputs. In this case the inputs are monitored; the results are evaluated by means of the tools and techniques and the detected nuisances are controlled and heads to the outputs.

Besides the key outputs of project monitoring and controlling there are also outputs which are common for all knowledge areas. These outputs will be shortly repeated. Afterwards, the knowledge areas will be discussed and outputs listed using the example of **project scope management**:

- Project communications management
- Project risk management and
- Project procurement management.
- Project scope management

- Project time management
- Project cost management
- Project quality management
- Project human resource management

All other knowledge areas – communication, risk, procurement, quality, and human resources, depend on or affect the three key points – cost, scope and time.

5.4.1 Common Outputs for all Knowledge

The key outputs for all common knowledge areas can also be outputs of project execution. These outputs are requested changes, recommended corrective actions and updates to applicable plans and processes.

During the execution of the process, change requests often occur. A process to handle changes is normally integrated into the project management plan. All members, project manager, team members, suppliers, sponsors and other stakeholders of the project can formally and informally request changes.

5.4.2 Recommended Corrective Action

Another important aspect which can be applied to every knowledge area is the outcome of recommended corrective action. Before recommending a corrective action, you first have to identify what has to   be corrected. Not only for quality improvements but also for other improvement techniques such as benchmarking, audits and cause-and-effect diagrams can be used. These techniques indicate what has to be corrected.

Also, updating project plans with respect to business processes is applicable for all knowledge areas. Thus it is important to get the information updates to the right person at the right time and in an appropriate format. For that matter, the information distribution is managed through improved communications. Every company uses its own samples for updating. These assets include guidelines, information, financial and management systems. Different media can be applied to improve communication.

Besides the normal media, instant messaging, webcasts, web-based courses and project blogs are used more and more often by project teams.

Project Scope Management

Project scope management concerns the project and includes all the work required, and only the work required, to complete the project successfully. It defines exactly what is and what is not included in the project scope e.g. key outputs and deliverables expected by the customer. It is very difficult to create an adequate project scope and minimize scope changes during the project. At the end of a project its scope is measured against the planned requirements. Therefore, all actions of the project must be well integrated to ensure the delivery of the predefined project specifications. Project scope can be seen as the fundamental basis for project planning and execution. Without clarity of scope, projects can encounter a large number of difficulties including scope creep, lack of support, inability to satisfy customer needs, inability to reach conclusion and the like. To manage these possibilities of failure it is necessary to install change control management, which is primarily concerned with the following issues:

- Identifying factors which create changes and make those changes beneficial
- Determining the occurrence of scope changes
- Managing changes when and if they occur

Change control processes include the implementation of changes within other management processes (e.g. time control, cost control, quality control, etc.). To consider all those factors, it is necessary to have a detailed process plan to implement scope change control correctly. Figure 5-3 illustrates how the process itself can be classified into categories of input, tools & techniques and outputs.

Inputs

The input scope describes the necessary data for the implementation of scope control. That data usually results from former project phases containing important data concerning the project plan or the progress.

Additionally, it is necessary to review the project scope statement which can be seen as a first step in controlling the project scope. It describes the project's deliverables and the work required to create those deliverables. The project scope statement also provides a common understanding of the project scope among all project stakeholders and describes the project's major objectives. It also enables the project team to perform more detailed planning. Further, it guides the project team's work during execution and provides the baseline for evaluating whether requests for changes or additional work are contained within or outside the project's boundaries. According to fig 5-3, the further inputs are the work breakdown structure, the performance report, the change request and the scope management plan.

Tools & Techniques

Tools and techniques use the previously mentioned inputs to apply certain processes which lead to the scope change control and monitoring. The following aspects are important to implementation of those processes:

Scope change control system: This system is documented in the project scope management plan and defines the procedures by which the project scope can be changed. The system includes the documentation, tracking systems, and approval levels necessary for authorizing changes. The scope change control system is integrated with any overall project management information system (PMIS). Such a system allows the gathering, integration and dissemination of the outputs of all project management processes. It is a very powerful tool to guide and support a projects through all its phases; a tool which provides both manual and automated system support to control project scope.

Performance measurement: Project performance measurements are used to assess the magnitude of scope variation. There are several techniques of performance reporting which can be used to assess project status or progress including:

- Variance analysis concerning areas of scope, quality, etc.
- Trend analysis over a time period with an eye on performance improvement or deterioration

- Earned value analysis for calculating the key values for each activity: budgeted cost of work scheduled (BCWS), actual cost of work performed (ACWP), budgeted cost of work performed (BCWP)

Important aspects of project scope control include determining the cause of variance relative to the scope baseline (including the project statement and WBS) and deciding whether corrective action is required.

Additional planning: Change requests from the input affect the project scope and require modifications of the WBS and WBS dictionary, the project scope statement, and the project scope management plan. These change requests can cause inevitable updates and modifications to components of the project management plan.

Outputs

Project Scope Changes: If the change requests have an effect upon the approved project scope and WBS, then the project scope statement is revised and reissued to reflect the approved changes. The updated project scope statement becomes the new project scope baseline for future activities. Such changes often require adjustments in other project objectives like cost, time, quality, etc. Project statement changes have to be fed back through the whole planning process where technical and planning documents are upgraded to the new status. Stakeholders have to be notified about those changes as well.

Corrective action: A recommended corrective action is any step recommended to bring expected future project performance in line with the project management plan and project scope statement. Therefore, it has to eliminate the cause of a detected non-conformity and prevent recurrence. Correction relates to containment and corrective action relates to the root cause of the variance.

Lessons learned: Lessons learned is used to refer to the specific records to analyze what went right and what went wrong in a project. The causes of variances, the reasoning behind the corrective action chosen, and other types of lessons learned from project scope change control are documented and updated in the historical database of the organizational process assets. Therefore, the organization benefits from the experience gained from a particular project and this will form the base knowledge which can be used for the current project and other upcoming projects to avoid the same variance occurrences and indicate the best way to deal with these. Lessons learned can be seen as a continuous improvement in organizations regarding project management.

Scope Change Management Process

Every project is specific and all of them have different specifications to achieve. Therefore, it is difficult to assign a general process on how to manage scope changes. Table 5-1 gives an example for control change management processes as described by Tennstepp.2 Such processes are usually implemented in the project management plan which is defined during the scope definition work step. The size of projects is the major factor in determining the appearance of scope change processes. Usually small projects have smaller scopes where changes also occur with smaller impacts and can be performed quickly.

The output of scope change control will have impacts on several processes and issues of the complete project. These impacts might occur as updates and lead to additional unplanned working activities which will further extend the scope of the project.

This shows how changes are managed when they occur and which people are responsible for the activities and decision making. Changes have to pass several validity levels until they finally become approved. Primarily it's the project manager, then the client manager and finally the project sponsor who approves the changes and implements the scope modification.

Sometimes small change requests face big change resistance. The client and other project team members may consider this to be an unnecessary overhead for such small decisions.

How should small change requests be managed? The following techniques can help to validate small changes:

- Batching of small requests: Instead of visiting the sponsor ten times for small scope changes, you batch them all together and see the sponsor once. This means that you keep track of the small scope changes, their business value and their impact on the project.
- Project Manager Discretion: This assumes that the project is on or ahead of schedule, and that the changes do not make the project exceed the agreed-upon cost or duration. In this case it may make sense for the project manager and client manager to be given discretion to approve small scope change requests.
- Scope Change Contingency Budget: Some organizations allocate a scope change contingency budget to handle small changes. In certain levels of scope change you may be allowed to allocate a percentage of the total project contingency budget to account for this level of change.

In the case of a scope change contingency budget, it might lead to pressure from the project manager to use the contingency budget to absorb additional requirements (or extra work) instead of making a formal change request. Further there should be a freeze on scope change requests in the last phase of a project. There comes a time in a project where it just doesn't make sense to make additional changes or absorb additional requirements. Not only are new changes expensive to implement, they are a distraction to the project team. With a scope freeze they can concentrate on and deliver the current solution.

It is important that the project sponsor approves changes. Even when the project team and the end users are the final users and know how important change might be, they cannot approve them. Only the project sponsor has the right to approve a change, because he is the one who can allocate the necessary resources and budget, and if the change is important enough the sponsor will approve it. A similar problem is the accountability in scope change management processes where everything should be performed according to Table 5-1. If for instance team members perform scope changes and the project is not ready on time or within budget they should know that they are accountable for this and could face consequences.

In cases where several organizations are involved in the project it is helpful to determine a change control board of decision makers, who approve change requests. Here it is necessary to clarify who is on the board, meeting frequency, reaction in emergencies and finally how they reach decisions, e.g. consensus, majority, unanimous, etc.

In cases where change requests are not approved by the sponsor, it is useful to capture them on a backlog list. After the project is finished, these requests can be implemented as an update when the time has come and the funding is available.

Schedule control provides tools and methods to identify variances to the planned project schedule. As soon as a baseline is established it can be compared to the actual project status and makes it possible to identify delays to important events. As time planning is one of the essential categories in project planning it is crucial to install schedule control to ensure your planned schedule milestones and performance.

Scope control can be seen as the comprehensive category which contains information and specifications about all other knowledge areas. The baseline for scope control is therefore the project specification which includes all data to the subsidiary knowledge areas. Therefore, changes in any other category e.g. schedule or quality affects scope, which can be seen as the major project summary.

5.5 Conclusion

For a project to be successful it is crucial to have a reliable progress and performance measurement system, otherwise no project member will know what the project status is. For effective project control it is essential to measure the progress of the project against the project plan. The project manager needs to be aware of what is going on, so he or she can take corrective action. In general, all projects vary from the plan and all schedules change.

Effective progress measurement helps to identify the variances. A good progress control plan or performance indicators are some tools which give a good overview of the overall status of the project and indicates, for example, the project's costs and schedule. However, the best information system does not automatically result in good control. Control requires the project manager to use information to steer the project through rough waters. Control and Gantt charts are useful vehicles for monitoring (time) performance.

Performance indicators should be meaningful and relevant to the project. They will be a good tool with which to monitor the project performance. To use performance indicators effectively a reliable system for data collection is required. It is a good approach if the original project staff members are replaced, because new team members can get the key data through the performance indicators. However, this is only one of several tools which can be used during project preparation, implementation and evaluation. It does not replace good time planning, economic, financial and cost-benefit analysis.

The ability to influence cost decreases with time, so real-time reports identifying adverse cost trends can greatly assist the project manager in getting back on budget and on schedule. The knowledge areas described by Duncan and Schwalbe provide a detailed analysis regarding cost, scope and time concerning a project. Without effective progress measurement it is difficult to accomplish the project's goals, therefore it is important that the project control and the collection of data are seen as an essential part of project management.

6 Risk Management

6.1 Introduction

Risk management plays an important part within project management. Inadequate risk management could have an impact whether the project will succeed or fail. To get an idea of what risk management is, what it means and how to use it as a tool for success, everybody can ask himself or herself the question:

What is a risk?

This easy question already shows that risk can be rather difficult to define as expectations are focused on the future and therefore, a lot of uncertainties could come into play. Additionally, these uncertainties could result in an outcome that is either more positive or more negative than expected. So it might be better to start with a definition of uncertainties:
Uncertainties = Threats + Opportunities

- Threats are events that have a negative impact on any result.
- Opportunities are events that have a positive impact on results; and
- Uncertainty encompasses the complete range of positive and negative impacts;

Literature often describes risk as" the possibility of suffering harm, loss or danger". Although one is usually not familiar with that definition we have an instinctive sense of risk. Everybody is confronted with risks in day-to-day activities. For example, we could be seriously injured in a car accident if the seat-belts are not fastened. If we are smoking too many cigarettes the possibility of dying of cancer is much higher than for a non-smoker. It is not our nature to think about all the possible risks that may affect us, but risks definitely shape our behaviors. If we want to cross the street, parents have told us to always look both ways before placing a foot onto the street.

Also, in every project there is the possibility for threats and benefits which may affect the success and/ or completion of a project. In our common understanding we associate a risk with being a problem but this is not right. A risk is not a problem until it really occurs. It is more a recognition that a possible problem might occur in the future.

By keeping that in mind the project manager is able to avoid risks by initiating adequate countermeasures. Project risks are those which can cause a project to be delayed or to exceed the planned budget. The field risk management deals with both – positive and negative – aspects of risk. But generally the project team is only concerned with the safety aspects of a project. Therefore, very often the negative consequences are the focus of risk management.

6.2 Risk Management

Risk management is a procedure to minimize the adverse effect of a possible financial loss by:

1) Identifying potential sources of loss;
2) Measuring the financial consequences of a loss occurring and
3) Using controls to minimize actual losses or their financial consequences.

The purpose of monitoring all project risks is to increase the value of each single activity within the project. The potential benefits and threats of all factors connected with these activities have to be ordered and documented. If the project team is aware of the importance of the risk management process, the probability of success will be increased while at the same time failure will become unlikely.

Risk identification is not solely done by the project manager. All relevant stakeholders are involved in keeping an eye on all risks that matter. Generally, the risk identification sessions should include as many as the following participants:

- Project team
- Risk management team
- Subject matter experts from other parts of the company
- Customers and end-user
- Other project managers and stakeholders
- Outside experts

The participants may vary but the project team should always be involved because they are dealing with the project every day and therefore need fresh information at any time. Outside stakeholders and experts could provide objective and unbiased information for the risk identification step and are therefore an essential part.

Risk identification has to be done throughout all project phases. If it is treated like a one-time event, then the whole project runs the risk of overlooking new emerging problems. The process starts in the project initiation phase where the first risks are identified. In the planning stage the project team determines risks and mitigation measures and documents them. In following stages of resource allocation, scheduling and budgeting the associated reserve planning is also documented.

After the initial phase of risk identification, all the risks have to be managed until the project is closed or terminated. New risks will occur as the project matures and the outer and inner environment of the project changes. Should risk probability increase or should the risk becomes real, it is time for the project manager to respond to it. The project team and manager have to think about the problem and develop strategies to deal with the impact of the problem. All the re-planning actions can mean a change to the baseline of budget, schedule and resource planning which affect the completion of the project.

How the project team will deal with project risks is clearly defined in the early stages of the project, then documented in the project plan and will be executed appropriately during the lifetime cycle of the project. Figure 6.1 illustrates the risk management process.

6.3   Risk Identification

Risk identification is the first and most important step because it builds the basis for all subsequent steps. The risk identification step is very similar to a transformation process.
In the beginning you have inputs and in the end you have a result or simply an output. In the middle step there are tools and techniques to fulfil the transformation process as shown in figure 6-2.

For the first input for risk, external and internal factors of the project environment have to be considered. External factors could be described as attributes of the environment whereas internal factors are attributes of the (project) organization itself. Typical examples for external factors are:

- Economic conditions

- Social, legal or regulatory trends
- Political climate
- Competition – international or domestic
- Fluctuation in demand
- Criminal or terroristic activities

Typical examples of internal factors are:

- Internal culture
- Staff capabilities/numbers
- Capacity
- Systems and technology
- Procedures and processes
- Communication effectiveness
- Leadership effectiveness
- Risk appetite

Information from prior projects usually records experience, developments, hints, failures and risks of those former projects which are now useful in helping to identify risks in the new project. The end documentation from recent projects ("lessons learnt") is a first step for gathering structured information. If kept in an (electronic) archive it is very useful in the preparation of future projects. If you start to review these documents at the beginning of a project it may lead to ideas on how you can improve your project and the organization of the project itself.

The project management plan is a formal and approved document which serves the project manager as a guideline in project execution and control. The project plan includes planning, assumptions and decisions, sets the communication ways among all stakeholders and records the approved scope, cost and schedule baselines.

The risk identification step requires that every relevant stakeholder has a complete understanding of the project. Only then are you able to consider the project from different perspectives and identify risks you wouldn't be able to identify without reading it.

Within the Tools & Techniques step you start with the documentation review to analyze information that already exists in a written form. In project management it is the project plan and the planning documents:

- Project charter
- Project scope
- Work breakdown structure (WBS)
- Project schedule
- Cost estimates
- Resource plan
- Procurement plan
- Assumptions list
- Constraints list

Usually you start the reviewing with the prior project files. With this technique you are trying to get an answer to the question: "Is the project really realistic in terms of budget, scope and schedule?"

Several information gathering methods can be used to identify risks related to the project. The major three used are:

Brainstorming, this is a general information-gathering and creativity technique which helps to identify risks and possible solutions for them. In a brainstorming session a group of team members and subject matter experts are "brainstorming" about possible outcomes and sources of risk. The ideas are generated under the leadership of a facilitator.
The brainstorming meeting should be done without interruptions and judgments or criticism of ideas. Very often the ideas are built on other ideas. In the end each identified risk will be categorized and its description will be sharpened. The goal of brainstorming is to obtain a comprehensive list of project risks.

The risk breakdown structure displays an organized description of any known project risks, arranged by a number of categories and their characteristics in the vertical branches. Usually it will show all of the risks and their possible causes.

The **SWOT analysis** is also used to define possible risks. In the 1960s and 1970s Albert Humphrey carried out research at Stanford University using data from 500 U.S. public corporations, and from this data he developed the SWOT analysis.

SWOT is an abbreviation and looks for strengths, weaknesses, opportunities and threats. Often SWOT is used as a basis for brainstorming. By defining strengths and opportunities, ideas of known or predictable weaknesses and threats will come to mind.

SWOT can be used for companies, their departments and divisions as well as for individual people. An advantage of SWOT analysis is that it is simple and relatively cheap except the time needed for it. It helps in generating new ideas.
On the other hand, the advantage is also the disadvantage as the easiness means that there is no detailed information about how to reach an objective or how important a threat is. A careful use of the outcome of the SWOT analysis is therefore highly recommended.

These tools and techniques help the project manager to gather relevant information, analyze it and identify risks and opportunities for the aim of the project, its scope, cost and budget. The information will then be stated on the so-called risk report/register, which is the main output of the risk identification step.

The risk report/register includes all identified risks and their description, risk categories, their causes, the probability of an occurrence, the single impacts of certain risks, possible responses, and their root causes. The whole risk identification process has four main entries on the risk register:

- Lists of identified risks – Identified risks with their root causes and risk assumptions are listed
- List of potential responses – Potential responses identified here will serve as inputs to the risk response planning process
- Root causes of risk – Root causes of risk are fundamental conditions which cause the identified risk
- Updated risk categories – The process of identifying risks can lead to new risk categories being added

As learnt from the previous points of risk identification, this step can comprise checklists of possible risks, surveys, meetings and brainstorming, reviews of plans, different analysis and so on. To do this appropriately requires a detailed knowledge of the organization and the project, the market in which it operates, the legal, social, political and cultural environment in which it operates, as well as the development of a clear understanding of the strategic and operational objectives the organization has, including factors critical to its success and the threats and opportunities related to the achievement of these objectives.

The risk identification should be done in a methodical way. This has to be done to ensure that all important activities and possible consequences related to these activities are identified.
It is also possible to outsource the whole risk management process but an in-house approach seems to be more effective when some conditions are fulfilled. First, the communication channels should be well-defined and consistent and processes and tools should be well coordinated.

6.4   Risk Analysis

The basis of risk analysis is the above explained risk identification. Risk analysis covers a complete and continuous evaluation which should be realized quantitatively as well as qualitatively for all identified risks. The goal is to detect possible interrelationships and enable the project manager to identify a kind of importance order, also called prioritizing. Furthermore, the consequences for the project itself and the organizational goals can be identified. The evaluation of the risks should meet the following demands:

- Objectivity: The reference to the special market should be taken into consideration to make the objectivity practicable. For internal risks a subject evaluation is often necessary.
- Comparability: The evaluation of risks should lead to comparable results. Therefore, the organization should use consistent and standardized methods and data.
- Quantification: By means of quantification the organization is able to detect deviation from the targeted goal.

- Consideration of interdependencies: In practice this is the hardest part of risk assessment. Effects like compensation and interdependencies can emerge. Not realizing connections between risks and their meaning for the department and possibly for the whole organization can be a big risk. That is why the project team should consider carefully what a risk and
- the reaction to it can mean not only for the team but for the whole organization as a good solution for one department can mean a problem for another department.

The most commonly used technique for risk analyzing is the so-called scenario analysis. This simply consists of the probability of the event and the impact this would have on the project.
The scenario analysis is part of many more approaches to the analysis of risks, for example in the matrix, the failure mode and effects analysis (FMEA) or the program evaluation and review technique (PERT).

To do a risk evaluation properly it should be defined first which levels will be used for evaluating the risks. For example, there should be ranges between 1 and 5 to give the impact or the likelihood a certain "size". If one wants a more detailed evaluation there could also be a range between 1 and 20. If one wants the evaluation to be more exact, there could also be a more exact classification of what a 'very low impact' means. This could be described by letters and for probability or affected costs, percentages could be stated for the different evaluation levels (see figure 6.3).

The evaluation form can be filled in jointly or with the help of an expert. Common techniques are versatile and range from exact point estimations to workshops.

Beside the most probable case, also the worst and the best cases are estimated. To make the risk analysis more demonstrative the organization can use the matrix to show the importance of several risks. The matrix shows two aspects of the considered risk: the impact it would have and the probability of its occurrence. A very often used matrix has 5 times 5 fields, each with another value of probability and impact (see Figure 6.4). As each combination has another meaning for the project, according to this the matrix is divided into a green, a yellow and a red zone. As known from traffic lights the red zone, representing the major risks, means nothing good. The yellow color stands for moderate and the green fields for minor risks. As one can see, the red zone is arranged on the right-hand side and the green zone on the left, where the impact is lower. In between the yellow zone can be found. The red zone goes very deep into the probability menu because the impact is still so high although the probability is low. In general, one can say that the impact is more important, as this comparison shows: 10% probability of losing 1 Mio. € is considered to be a more serious risk than a 90% probability of losing 1000 €.

With the help of this matrix the project manager can prioritize the risks so that he knows which risks should be addressed particularly and at first. Prioritization also helps to adopt the given means reasonably, which is very important as all resources in project management such as material, financial means, human resources and time are limited.

The FMEA (Failure mode and effects analysis) model is similar to the matrix but extends the impact and probability by the detection possibility, meaning how hard it is to actually realize the occurring risk. The equation enlarged with detection is:

$$\text{Impact} \times \text{Probability} \times \text{Detection} = \text{Risk Value}$$

To make the equation work each of the dimensions has to be evaluated by a five-point scale. Detection describes the ability of the project team to detect that the risk is threatening. On the 1 to 5 scale, "1" would mean easy to detect and "5" that the detection would probably only take place when it is considered too late.
The product of the data would have a range between 1 and 125.

'1' shows the risk has a low probability, an impact of level 1 and would be easy to detect. At the other extreme the result '125' would show that the team had to handle a high-impact risk whose probability is high and nearly impossible to detect. That would mean consideration has to be given whether to start the project or not if the risk could not be mitigated or transferred. All in all, the range between 1 and 125 can be used to define the hazardous nature of a risk.

PERT (Program evaluation and review technique) was developed within the framework of the U.S. Navy's Polaris-Project. Nobody knew how long it would take to produce the parts for the rocket. There were many new parts coming from R&D. To solve the problem of planning, the team asked all suppliers to estimate the duration of production. It is assumed that with the help of the program evaluation and review technique the construction of the Polaris rocket was accomplished after two years, which is about 45% earlier than first estimated.

PERT is similar to the critical path method (CPM) known from the scheduling theory. The methods were developed at nearly the same time. The difference is that CPM uses the most frequent duration and is used for standardized projects. In contrast to that, PERT is used for projects with high uncertainty and little experience. PERT is utilized to compute the probability of meeting different project durations.

PERT is useful as it provides the expected project completion time and the probability of the completion before a specified date. Furthermore, it helps in finding out the activities which may have slack time and those that can lend resources to critical activities. Disadvantages are that the estimates can be somewhat subjective and also depend upon the experience of the project members. Furthermore, the beta distribution might not always match the reality. It is said that PERT often underestimates the project completion time because other paths than assumed before can become critical paths if the related activities become late.

6.5 Risk Response

After having collected all data for the risk control, a risk might occur once. As a result, the project manager has to decide how to react to it.
The literature defines five main alternatives between which one can choose: mitigate, avoid, transfer, share or retain the risk.

To mitigate the risk means a reduction of the impact and the possibility of risk occurrence. This is something one can do before starting the whole project. If one detects a risk and knows this risk could be reduced, there are two alternatives: the probability of the occurrence could be reduced or the impact the occurred risk would have. Normally, first an attempt is made to reduce the probability and then the impact. The latter is more expensive and perhaps not even necessary to consider if probability could be reduced significantly.

Two terms known especially from engineering projects are testing and prototyping. By testing and prototyping one can test the project in a smaller format with less risk and thereby detect possible failures and problems. With the help of this, the team can prepare for these problems or even eliminate them before starting the real project work.

Two things that cannot be mitigated easily are cost and time, because money is used up and the days are numbered. But risk management has a solution for this: budget reserves and time buffers. Before this is done one always has a kind of safety ratio. This ratio is often directly related to the experience gained from recent projects.

Avoiding risk is already a more drastic approach as the whole project plan might be changed to avoid the particular risk. One should consider carefully whether particular risk warrants changing the plan. An example of avoiding a risk could be using well known technology instead of new, experimental, technology.

With the risk transfer, the risk is just moved but not eliminated or dampened. One very common approach is outsourcing which is done far in excess in some industries. Then the contractor has to take the risk. Beside the fact that of course the risk transfer will cost money – as the contractor also has to include the risk possibility in his pricing – it could be challenging to ensure the subcontractor is able to deal with the risk.

Also, a well-known approach to transferring risks is contracting insurance. This may work well for some specific cases but for project management in general it is not really the right approach. Contracting insurance for a project can be used for low-probability and high-impact events. As these are somehow often Acts of God they are more easily defined (e.g. an earthquake), but for day-to-day business risk insurances they are too expensive and the risks could not be described exactly enough.

Sharing risk, as the name says, means that different parties share the risks of the same project. One well known example is Airbus – from the aircraft industry. Airbus allocated risk to the R&D departments over different countries like France, Britain and Germany.

Another kind of sharing of risk is signing a BOOT contract. BOOT is an abbreviation for "Build-Own- Operate-Transfer", meaning the project organization is building the plant and after that the organization is the owner until the operations are running smoothly and the whole check-up is done. Only if all these steps are successful is the ownership transferred to the client.

Sharing risks is also one possible way to save money. The approach is often used in the field of logistics. With combining the ideas of the subcontractor with the project team parent's organization ideas a big improvement could be made, but to reach a level of teamwork where these procedures work, both sides should gain advantages from this relationship. This is also one reason why partnerships can emerge. Then the relationship is good enough to work together closely. Both sides are taking the risk and the benefits coming from new ideas are most probably equal by that stage.

The last option, retaining a risk, seems a bit strange at first sight that, but there are cases where retaining and accepting the risk can be the easiest way to handle it. The possibility of such events occurring is often so low that the risk could be accepted. More often, the impact of the risk is very low and it is easier to buffer it with financial help and just keep on working.

With the help of buffers and reserves some risks could be taken as they appear. It could be easier to take the risk instead trying unsuccessfully to transfer or reduce the risk. In a few cases the occurrence of the event could be ignored totally.

A contingency plan provides a plan which is fulfilled if one of the known risks becomes reality. With the help of that plan the action that is to be followed is already clear before the risk appears. That helps us to stay calm and get step by step to a solution which can be e.g. reducing or weakening the impact of the event. The contingency plan should then say what, when and where which actions are to be taken. With the help of the contingency plan the manager who has to deal with the occurring problem does not have to invent a solution on the spot, which in any event would be a low quality solution, still taking time to find. It is much easier if one can look into the contingency plan where the steps are described after they have been well thought out during the project planning phase. The availability of a contingency plan can significantly increase the chances for project success.

At first sight it might seem easy: just plan the risks and it's done but there are some conditions one has to consider. First of all, proper documentation of the steps is necessary. Within that documentation cost estimations and the probable source should be named. Furthermore, the involved teams should agree on the plan and the allocation of tasks should be clear. All these steps should be followed to ensure all team members know what to do and are committed to the work, especially in case of an emergency.

Having a contingency plan is absolutely necessary. Otherwise a risk might slow the managerial response and any decisions made under pressure will likely be poor and potentially dangerous and costly.

One good way to follow all these instructions is to make a note of this information within a so-called risk response matrix. Still, there is a more extreme possibility left which one has to think of during risk contingency planning. There is the possible eventuality that the risk remains after a risk response as per the contingency plan.

6.6 Risk Control

The very last step in the whole risk management process is risk control. Included in this step are executing the risk response strategy, monitoring and triggering events, initiating contingency plans, and continuously watching for new risks.
In the risk control portion the change in management systems is also an essential part. During the project there might be changes in scope, budget, and schedule which the project manager has to deal with.

It is also the duty of the project manager to monitor all possible risks in just the same way as he/she is interested in the project progress. Risk assessment and updating should be part in every status meeting and progress report system. Also, the project team should have the constant awareness that unpredictable risks may occur.
But this is not the usual case in every project. Team members are not always willing to find out new risks and problems. If the actual organization culture is one where mistakes are punished by the management, then it is clear that the team members will be reluctant to speak up about these topics because they think these problems might reflect their bad performance. The tendency to suppress such important information is higher when the responsibilities are unclear and the team is under great time pressure from the top management to finish the project in within a short timeframe.

So it is the duty of the project manager to create an environment in which all team members feel free to raise concerns and admit mistakes. This should be the standard in every project, because hiding risks or denying problems is not good for the future success of the company. Everybody should be encouraged to identify problems and new risks and therefore the project manager has to have a positive attitude toward risk.

In very complex and huge projects the risk identification and assessment step has to be repeated on a regular basis. Outside stakeholders and experts should be brought into the discussion so that they also can review the actual risk profiles of the project.

Another useful key success factor is the assignment of responsibility for every identified risk. This step could be very complicated in the case where multiple organizations are involved in the project. Then nobody really feels responsible for dealing with that occurred risk. The responsibility is passed on to one another.by saying: "this is not my work." This mentality is very dangerous for the whole project.

So it is very important that the responsibility for each identified risk is assigned by the mutual agreement of all relevant stakeholders so that everybody knows who is dealing with what. If the whole risk management process is not formalized, the response and the responsibility for certain risks will simply be ignored.

Project audits usually play an important part in the Risk Response Control. An audit can be defined as a systematic and independent analysis. The term "audit" has its origin in the Latin language. The Latin word "audire" means "hear", so quality audit is a "quality hearing".

With the help of audits, it can be checked if quality-related work and the results which are gained from that work conform to the standards and the planned requirements. It checks whether the work is done economically and rationally. The main aim of the audits is the discovering of weak points and risks inside an organization or project. A big advantage of audits is the ability to check quality-related issues and workflow in a very good way. A disadvantage is the high time demand for the preparation of the paperwork and the training of the employees. However, audits only allow a short snap-shot of the visible situation. Some employees see this as a control over the work they performed and may come to resent the auditor.

Every audit results in an audit report. Internal reports must contain, for example, the basic information and procedures for the evaluation and observations in terms of project documentation or personnel qualification. Of course non-conformities also have to be reported. This is necessary for the next audit in order to check if corrective actions have been considered. Furthermore, there has to be a list of participants in an audit report.

Another major part of the risk control process is establishing a change management system. It is commonplace that the project will not materialize the way you originally planned it. There are many sources and causes of changes that possibly could affect your project and its course. Usually you could categorize these changes into one of the following categories:

- Changes in Scope: For example, the project customer wants to implement an additional feature or a change in design which really represents a big challenge.
- Implementation of contingency plans: In this situation a risk really occurred. Now counteractive measures have to take. These actions need resources in terms of cost and schedule and so represent a change to the baseline.
- Improvement changes by project team members: For example, a change in suppliers. A new supplier can deliver more cheaply in the same quality.

All changes usually represent big challenges to the whole team and project manager. Often changes to the project are not avoidable and therefore a well-defined change review and control process in the early stages of a project is required. These control process include reporting, controlling and recording changes to the baseline of the project. Most change control systems are designed to fulfil the following criteria:

- Identify proposed changes
- List expected effects of proposed changes on schedule and budget
- Review, evaluate, and approve or refuse changes formally
- Negotiate and resolve conflicts of change, conditions and cost
- Communicate changes to parties affected
- Assign responsibility for implementing change
- Adjust master schedule and budget
- Track all changes that are to be implemented

In general, stakeholders and the communication plan, which is defined in advance, will determine the communication and decision-making process to be used in order to make any changes to the project. The decision-making process may vary between bigger and smaller projects. On larger projects it could be that, for instance, when you want to change important requirements of the project you need multiple sign-offs from different stakeholder whereas switching a single supplier could be done by the project manager himself because he has the authorization to do so.

Never underestimate the impact of changes to the project. Very often several solutions have adverse effects on the so far completed project. Therefore, all changes have to be assessed by people with the appropriate knowledge and perspective in their respective fields.

Every accepted change must be integrated into the plan of record through changes in the WBS (work breakdown structure) and baseline schedule. The plan of record is the current reference in terms of schedule, costs and scope. If the change control system is not integrated with the WBS and baseline, sooner or later the project plan and control system will become unworkable. The key success factor for the change control system is to document every single change occurring. Benefits of these requirements are:

- Inconsequential changes are discouraged by the formal process
- Costs of changes are maintained in a log
- Integrity of the WBS and performance measures is maintained
- Allocation and use of budget and management reserve funds are tracked
- Responsibility for implementation is clarified
- Effect of changes is visible to all parties involved
- Implementation of change is monitored
- Scope changes will be quickly reflected in baseline and performance measures

Change control is an important part of the project. As the project matures there must be a person or group who is responsible for approving the changes, keeping the documents updated, and communicating all changes to the relevant stakeholders. Success depends heavily on keeping the change control process updated.

6.7 Conclusion

After having read this chapter you have now likely gained a basic understanding of what risk management is and how it works. The conclusion must be: **Undertake Risk Management!**

It has nearly only benefits. The effort involved in creating a well-defined and well-running risk management system is enormous, but the price is definitely worth paying.

If the project manager and all relevant stakeholders undertake risk management, it will add value to each single activity and therefore to the whole project. Improvements are:

- Provides a framework for the whole project in which activities happen in a consistent and controlled way
- Improves the decision-making process, supports the planning process and prioritization of each activity by having a complete understanding off all project-related activities and project opportunities and threats
- Reducing uncertainty within the project
- Securing or even increasing assets of the company
- Optimizing operational efficiency
- Developing and supporting the organization's knowledge base

Never forget: risk management is an ongoing process and many project managers learn their lesson the hard way. Remember, risk never sleeps.

7 Docs, Audit, Termination and Closure

7.1 Introduction

Projects undergo progressive elaboration by the development in steps and predictable increments that are tied to benchmarks, milestones and completion dates. This finite characteristic of projects stands in sharp contrast to processes, or operations, which are permanent or semi-permanent functional work to repetitively produce the same product or service. In practice, the management of these two systems is often found to be quite different, and as such requires the development of distinct technical skills and the adoption of separate management philosophy. This chapter deals with essentials for a successful procedure; starting with the project documentation, showing the audit process and finishing with reasons and examples for the termination and the closure of a project.

7.2 Documentation

A clear documentation system and systematically laid down documentation simplifies the internal and external communications and facilitates project management, for example, in the case of the temporary absence or illness of someone in charge.

Documentation is essential for leading, defining, planning, organizing, controlling, and closing a project. Too much documentation is as much of a problem as too little. A balance must exist, depending largely on the size and importance of the project.

Good documentation serves as an excellent communication tool. It provides an audit trail for analysis and project reviews. It lends order and structure to the project by giving direction and setting parameters. It increases efficiency and effectiveness and it gives team members confidence, especially when things appear chaotic or there are too many unknowns.

Project documentation may consist of the following items and those marked in bold type, which play the most important roles, will be described in more detail:
- **Procedures**
- Flowcharts
- Forms
- Reports
- Memos

- **Project manual**
- **Project library**
- Newsletters
- History files

7.2.1 Procedures

For many projects, particularly large ones, procedures facilitate management. They help achieve efficiency by ensuring consistency of action. They improve effectiveness by ensuring that people achieve project goals. They reduce the learning curve by providing guidance on the "way things are done." Finally, they improve productivity because people with questions can refer to the documentation rather than interrupt other people.

Developing procedures is more than just writing words on paper. Regardless of ones' writing ability, one has to consider the following when developing procedures:

- Defining acronyms, the first time they appear and spelling out abbreviations at first use. The reader may not know what is meant.
- Defining special terms. The user needs to understand what is said.
- Avoiding clichés. They are a tired way of expressing what is meant.
- Checking for errors. They distract from the message and show sloppiness.
- Using positive expressions. Avoiding "do not" or "cannot" because such phrases create a mental block in the reader's mind.
- Using the active rather than the passive voice. The active voice is strong language; the passive voice is weak and reveals a tentative writer.
- Arguments should flow logically, such as from the "big picture" to the details, or vice versa.
- A chronological order should also be used.
- Track different versions. Assigning a version number to each and noting the date, so everyone uses the most recent version.

7.2.2 Project Manual

It is often useful to have certain information available, such as phone numbers and task listings. The project manual forms this basic but essential reference book for the project team. However, it does more than provide useful information. It is also a communication tool, enabling people to interact efficiently and effectively.

Ideally, the manual should be prepared early on and be maintained throughout the project cycle. The project manager as well as the sponsor and the steering committee should have ready access to it, either in hard copy or electronic form.

The following content is usually to be found in a project manual:

1) Organizational Chart of the project team
2) Up-to-date project scope
3) Project Manager's Project Control List
4) Project Control
    - Schedule
    - Meetings
    - Procurement
5) Cost Control (due to the confidential information nonpublic in all parts)
    - Labor cost information: The summary of labor cost for the most recent and two control periods.
    - Resources: The current copy of the project manager's resource charge report.
    - Cost to complete: The most recent project manager's projected cost to complete summary.
6) Financial Control:
    - Change order log: Copy of the current C/O Log.
    - Project Cost Code Summary: Current copy of the project cost code summary report.
7) Contracts
    - Summary of status of each contract amount and changes.
    - Subcontracts & Purchase Orders: Alphabetical insertion of project manager's copies of subcontracts. Each subcontract is to be preceded by the summary sheet.
8) Documentation:

- Project manager's project summary sheet (subcontract status)
- Document control logs
- Requests and changes Log
- Contracts
- Submittals log

7.2.3 The Project Library

Small and medium projects and especially multinational projects can involve an enormous document load. This load can vary from hundreds to thousands of documents. The way in which they are organized will affect the project in a number of ways. Misplacement of documents means spending time searching for them or even reproducing them. This causes loss of time, loss of revenue and demotivation of employees. These consequences can easily be avoided.

The basic principle of the Project Library is that all information is stored.

The project library, like the history files, stores information. The major difference is that the library contains more than project management information. The project library also stores company and project-specific policies and procedures, history files, newsletters, journal publications, and related books, and technical documentation.

Steps to set up the library:

- Identifying the contents, e.g., by interviewing team members for their suggestions.
- Determining the organization, e.g., arranging documents by title, code, or author.
- Controlling the removal of documents, e.g., by providing a check-in/check-out sheet.
- Determining the location of the library, e.g., providing a readily accessible site; the project manager also determines the procedures for accessing material.

Too much or too little documentation can negatively affect a project. The key is to have the right amount of documentation to satisfy the right needs. The content of documents should be current, clear, concise, and organized to be useful to team members. It has to be ensured that documentation is accessible to everyone, such as through a project manual or library.

7.3 Audit

An audit (lat. "Hearing") can be described as an evaluation of a person, organization, system, process, project or product. Audits are performed to ascertain the validity and reliability of information, and also provide an assessment of a system's internal control. The goal is to find out whether or not a project for example is "on time" or "out of budget". It is also used to find out if the project meets its specifications and is often part of the quality management of a company. In general, an audit is a tool to improve quality.

The audit may be a single occurrence or a repetitive activity, depending on the purpose and the results of both the audit and the product/service, process, project or management system concerned. A properly conducted audit is a positive and constructive process accomplished by qualified personnel.

Depending on the subject the "current status" is analyzed, or a comparison with the actual targets is done. Often an audit is used to find unspecified problems or potential for possible improvements. It helps prevent problems through the identification of activities likely to create problems. Problems generally arise from the inefficiency or inadequacy of the activity concerned.

Audits play an important role during installation, certification and running of management systems as well as for the evaluation of projects. Audits can be distinguished by different criteria:

By subject

- Financial
- Information

- Exactness, Validation
- Compliance
- Performance
- Goal reaching
- Economic efficiency
- System audit
- Product audit
- Process audit
- Project audit
- Quality audit
- Environmental
- etc.

By Auditor

- Internal audit (1st Party)
- Supplier audit (2nd Party)
- Certification audit (3rd Party)

Others

- Audit in relation to the certification of management systems
- Pre-audit to determine the possibility of certification (a so-called "friendly audit")
- Survey audit

7.3.1 Main Audit Types

Although many types of audits exist, basically all of them are based on one of three types. This distinction is made by the subject of the audit. These three subjects are: products (services), processes and systems. This leads to the basic audit distinction.

The Product Audit

The product audit examines a product or a service. In the case of a service the audit is called a service audit but the system is the same. The examined aspects in this audit are different attributes of the product e.g. packing or conformity with the set standards. The audit is made on the final product after the regular final inspection. This means the product is tested in the condition in which it would be delivered to the customer. So the audit can also include the evaluation of the logistics system which carries out the delivery. This audit type is more technical and could also include a destructive test of the product. The complete product characteristics should be examined. In addition to this, the audit should be made frequently.

The Process Audit

In this type of audit, a single process is examined. Usually only one work crew is involved in the evaluation. The process audit is used to find out whether or not the process is within the time limits and conforms to the specifications. This could also include examinations of the process environment and all single parameters which are important to the process such as temperature, pressure or accuracy. As well as special processes like welding or examinations, the resources of the process and the inputs and outputs are tested. This type of audit can also be part of the system audit.

The System Audit

The subject of interest in a system audit is the management system. To evaluate a management system every action or decision which has an influence, for example, on the quality program of the company has to be documented. Furthermore, this audit takes a look at everything that is influenced by the management (this is also necessary to evaluate the decisions made). Therefore, a system audit includes product and process audits as well as service audits and even looks at the company's internal departments such as purchasing or waste management.

Internal and External Audits

Another classification of audits is the distinction between internal and external Audits. Internal audits are "first-party" audits while external audits can be either "second-party" or "third-party".

The first-party audit is an internal audit. Its main attribute is that the auditors are employed by the examined company. It is important that the auditors are not concerned by the results of the audit. It is therefore useful that the auditors are part of a different department than the one examined. The reason for an internal audit is the measuring of weaknesses and strengths according to the company's own standards. This type of audit can also be outsourced. The advantage here is that the company's own workers can continue with their day-to-day business.

The second-party audit is more formal than the first-party audit. This is because it can have an influence on contracts (which this type of audit can be a part of) and on purchasing decisions. The audit is performed by external employees for example from the customer on a supplier. The evaluation itself takes into account the facilities, resources, personnel, etc. This audit is for example done before a contract is signed to ensure that the supplier is able to meet the requirements.

The main feature of the third-party audit type is the complete independence of the auditor. A third -party audit is performed by an external auditing company. As a result, no conflicts of interest can occur while an audit is performed. The goals of these audits are certifications, approvals or awards but also penalties or fines. As an example: The government does mandatory audits on safety in relevant industries like nuclear plants.

7.3.2   Motives of an Audit

Quality is defined as fitness for use, conformance to requirements and the pursuit of excellence. Even though the concept of quality has existed from early times, the study and definition of quality have been given prominence only in the last century. Over the past several years there have been many interpretations of what quality is, beyond the dictionary meaning of "general goodness". Other terms describing quality include "reduction of variation", "value added" and "conformance to specifications".
DIN ISO 9000:2000 defines Quality as the degree to which a set of inherent characteristics fulfils requirements. Simply stated, quality is meeting customer requirements. Others prefer to describe quality in terms of achieving customer satisfaction.

A system of quality management includes all activities of the overall management function that determine the quality policy, objectives and responsibilities and their implementation. A management system provides the means of establishing a policy and objectives and the means to achieve those objectives.

Auditing is part of the quality assurance function. It is important to ensure quality because it is used to compare actual conditions with requirements and to report those results to the management. Although audits are performed mostly to improve quality (with regard to the definition of the term "quality"), there are some concrete reasons to perform audits. The facts provided by an audit can be used to:

- Provide input for management decisions, so that problems and costs can be prevented or rectified.
- Keep management informed of actual or potential risks.
- Identify areas of opportunity for continual improvement.
- Asses personnel training effectiveness and equipment capability.
- Provide visible management support of the quality, environment and safety programs.
- Ensure ongoing compliance with and conformity to regulations and standards.
- Determine system and process effectiveness.
- Identify system and process inefficiencies.
- Improving business performance.

Preparation and Costs

One of the most important steps concerning audits is the right preparation. The main step here is defining clear objectives. Examples for those objectives are:

- Perform and present meaningfully (for the customer)
- Ensure regular performance of required audits and ensure frequent audits of critical functions
- Ensure that audits are performed only by trained, qualified, and independent auditors
- Promote a strong alliance between the audit function and the auditee
- Standardize the auditing process and form a basis against which to measure continual improvement of the audit program

- Support the objectives/strategies/goals of the organization
- Ensure project and operational safety and proper environmental stewardship
- Support management objectives for improving project performance

In addition to defining the objectives, and agenda a is needed as well as a clear definition of the responsibilities. Also the reasons for the audit must be clear for everyone involved. A simple tool which helps in successful auditing is a set of seven questions that need to be asked before starting:

1. Who performs and who participates in the audits?
2. What activity or system is being audited?
3. Where are the audits performed?
4. When are the audits performed?
5. Why are the audits performed?
6. What is the driving force behind the audit?
7. How is the audit performed?

Like every activity used to improve or measure a process, product or project, an audit generates costs. Those costs should be lower than the cost of the benefits. Although the benefits can't be estimated exactly before the audit (often because of the "unclear" result) the costs can be relatively clearly estimated. The costs are:

- The auditor's time spent preparing, performing, reporting, following up and closing the audit
- The Auditee's time spent participating in and following up on actions arising from the audit
- Overhead costs of materials, travel, accommodation, support staff and logistics

It should be mentioned that audit costs can rise enormously when performed by inappropriate personnel, meaning untrained auditors or people who are involved in the company or even in the examination process. The reason for this is the inability of that person to give constructive analyses. In most such cases the result is only destructive critique.

As mentioned earlier, the audit is not a single operation. It is a tool to improve quality and quality can always be improved. So the idea of the audit cycle is that is an ongoing process, which means that audits are performed from time to time. But audits should be connected to each other. Improvement starts when the results are compared. Also, the auditors become more skilled and maybe find potential improvements they did not see earlier. The goals can also change after a while, maybe because of new technical achievements or simply because of an environmentally change. If goals are changed the whole audit process has a new basis and needs to be repeated.

7.4 Project Termination

When hearing the term "project termination" most people think about the termination of a project caused by failure. But the term is not dependent upon the success of the project. It also happens that a successful project can end earlier than originally planned. But for most people the word "termination" has a negative meaning. This abstract will focus more on reasons and problems of termination than on the "normal" closure phase. Sometimes the term "termination" is used as an equivalent for "project closure". Another word is "close-out", also used as an equivalent. The term termination is used for an ending of a project before it was planned. If a project ends in the planned time it is mostly called project closure. Close-out in literature is often used as an "umbrella term". Project closure will be discussed later in this chapter.

7.4.1 Reasons for Termination

Termination of a project is predictable, but how is it terminated and when? It may have a deep and long lasting impact on the organization and its employees.

The success of projects to come may depend not only on the success of past ones, but also on how unsuccessful projects are treated by the organization and its stakeholders. Companies have the option of initiating various corporate projects with varying degrees of risk. If an organization chooses to accept greater risks, it should avoid disciplining members of projects that turn out to be unsuccessful. If team members believe they will be punished for participating in being a member unsuccessful projects, they might be less willing to terminate failed projects and may become unwilling to take a risk.

External and internal factors that influence the success or failure of projects will be identified and clustered. The importance of each factor identified varies by organization and project type. Organizing the termination process is in particular important when it has failed, because of the long-standing impact on future projects as well as the organization's image. Including project team members in the termination process will increase their commitment and loyalty, especially to the organization and to future projects. A post-audit report will be prepared at the end of a project that summarizes the project and provides recommendations on possible project approaches for similar tasks in the future. In a final step, as a project is terminated or completed it is important that senior management recognizes and rewards the contributions of the project team.

Several factors have direct influences on the usability of a planned or running project. All factors usually fall into one of the following categories. During the life of a project, the steering committee and the project management must examine these critical factors continually to ensure that it can still realize the initially set goals.3

Technology: The technological track of the project can have a major influence on its chance of success. steering committee and the project management must be able to value the technological path so that they can:

      a. measure the progress of the project;
      b. have a general idea of when breakthroughs can be expected;
      c. not become disappointed when the rapidity of development appears slow.

Organization: Organizational factors that can influence the practicability of a project include internal competition, executive support and the company's strategy. Internal competition, especially in critical situations like access to important funding or resources, will affect the project team's motivation. Also, as the number of projects increases, the more likely it is that one of them will end in failure. This mirrors a natural development of management support. Maintaining management's support in some projects is likely to be the single most important factor in influencing the success or failure of a project. Another factor extremely important is the compatibility of the project with the corporation's strategy. A project that no longer fits with the organization's objectives is usually dedicated to be terminated.

Market forces: The competition has a strong influence on the viability of new or planned projects. The value of a project can be reduced by the sudden availability of alternatives or competing technological innovations. Continuing to fund an outdated project can be avoided by maintaining communication between the marketing, manufacturing, and R&D departments.

Planning: Naturally, the firm's ability to manage a project will have a significant impact on its eventual success or failure. Central to this, of course, is the project plan, which should be exceptionally detailed. Difficulties which could threaten the schedule must be identified so that workable alternatives can be developed ahead of time. There will always be a basic, inherent level of uncertainty in every project; however, thorough planning can reduce most of these risks to an acceptable level. It is also important to note that the quality and level of planning for a project is frequently related to the level of experience of the project team. More experienced project teams tend to plan and organize more effectively.

The project team. As would be expected, the team plays a key role in the project's success or failure. The effectiveness of a team is, in turn, governed by the abilities of its project manager, the team's overall commitment and enthusiasm, and the co-operation of the team as a whole. That means the role of the project manager is the most critical.
He or she must be able to co-ordinate changing activities, resolve conflicts, and keep management informed and committed to the project – while also keeping the project on track.

The project team should also be relatively stable. Changing important team members at critical stages in the schedule can have a fatal effect. On the other hand, a new team member, if briefed properly, can provide a fresh approach to many problems.

Economic factors: These factors may have a significant influence on the project's ability to generate a minimum acceptable return on the organization's investment. While financial measures, such as return on investment (ROI), are not the only factors influencing success or failure, they do provide a measurement tool for evaluation. It is entirely possible that a project, which is on schedule and well within its budget, may be cancelled because of unrelated financial constraints dictated by the organization. When firms fail to achieve their desired level of profitability, they always have the option to re-evaluate ongoing projects and terminate those that are less viable or overly expensive.

Other: Miscellaneous factors that influence the success or failure of a project include new government regulations, problems with patent ownership, or new environmental concerns.

The key, of course, is being able to recognize if and when projects start to fail. To do this requires maintaining a feedback loop throughout the project cycle. And the effectiveness of the feedback loop depends upon a constant flow of quality information among the project manager, team members, the customer, and senior management.

7.4.2 Types of Project Termination

There are two types of project termination – "natural termination" and "unnatural termination". "Natural termination" reflects the fact that the aims of the project objective have been attained. "Unnatural termination" means that work on the project has stopped because the project constraints have been violated or the project objective has become irrelevant to the overall goals. There are four common ways for terminating a project:

1. Extinction
2. Addition
3. Integration

4. Starvation

The following are the most likely reasons for which a project may be terminated:

By Extinction

- The project has successfully completed the planned scope and the client has accepted it.
- It has been superseded by the external developments like technological advancement, market crisis etc.
- It has failed to achieve its goal.
- It no longer has the support of senior management.

By Addition

Termination by addition occurs when the project team becomes a new part of the parent organization. Resources are transferred to the new organizational unit, which is integrated into the parent organization. This type of project termination is typical for organizations with a project structure.

By Integration
The project is successfully completed. The project product is integrated into the operations of the client.

This is the most common mode and most complex operation. Termination by integration occurs when the project's resources, as well as its deliverables, are integrated into the parent organization's various units. This approach is very common in a matrix organization because most people involved in a project are also affiliated with one or more functional units. When the project terminates, team members are reintegrated into their corresponding units.

By Starvation

- The project is terminated by budget decrement.
- It is also known as withdrawal of "life support".
- The reason for this termination is generally to shadow the failure to accomplish the goals. This can save face for the senior management and avoid embarrassment.

Senior management is responsible for the decision to terminate. Before making a decision senior management should work closely with the project manager who is in charge of the project. The project manager should know the situation quite well. If he is a good project manager, he works closely with the project team and gets periodic feedback. So he should be able to give the management advice whether the project should be terminated or not.

There are also other "measurement methods" with which to decide if the project should be terminated or not. Before terminating, a final audit could verify the results to give senior management another source of advice.

7.4.3   Project Termination Problems

There are some problems caused by project termination. These can be divided into two groups. The first group covers the emotional problems. These problems can be divided again into two parts, problems with the staff and problems with the client. The staff might be afraid that they won't have future work. Project termination can also lead to some losses, for example loss of interest in the remaining task, loss of project-derived motivation or the loss of the team identity. You also might have some trouble with reassignment. Which people will be put together in which project?

On the other hand, there is the client. After a termination he might change his attitude, lose interest in the project, or won't ask the organization to take part in further projects. It also might be that the client will change his personnel: knowing that the project has already failed, the client might decide that people who worked on the project should change their position. This could lead to unavailability of key personnel.

The second group deals with physical problems. This group can also be divided into two smaller ones as shown in fig. 7-1.

A project may be cancelled for a variety of reasons, including lack of funding, technological obsolescence, changes in consumer trends, mergers and acquisitions, loss of the "champion", and negative cost/benefit relationships. Although the reasons may vary, the impact is frequently the same. Project cancellation can affect employee productivity, the reputation of the firm, and the value of the firm's stock. Although hardly any research on the topic of employee productivity and project cancellation has been done, experience suggests that a project team's perception of the cancellation may influence their productivity for the next several years. However, there are guidelines to help soften the impact of cancellation on the team. To begin with, it is essential that the project team is included in the cancellation process and should be made aware of the rationale behind the cancellation well before the official announcement. Moreover, this rationale should be consistent with the perceptions of the project team.

A study found eight factors which influenced whether an employee perceived the cancellation of a project negatively:

1. The rationale for cancellation.
2. Communication between management and the project team.
3. Careful planning for the cancellation process.
4. Strong management commitment and support for the project from its inception.
5. Effective planning and leadership of the project.
6. Prompt and comparable reassignment of project personnel.
7. Acknowledgment of the efforts of the project team.
8. Participation of the project team in the cancellation decision-making process.

As might be expected, the output and commitment of team members immediately before a project is cancelled, and for one or two months after the announcement, will be drastically reduced. This loss in productivity and commitment will be exacerbated if the project team perceives the cancellation negatively. Worse, the individual's commitment to the organization may depend upon his or her perception of the cancellation. Employees who view a cancellation in a more positive light will have higher levels of commitment than those who view it more negatively.

How a project is viewed within the organization is also very important. Because corporate resources can be very limited, projects that are perceived to be draining scarce resources tend to undercut morale. Other project teams envy the resources "squandered" on unproductive or failing projects. This, in turn, leads employees to question the wisdom of senior management, and reduces their productivity and level of commitment to the organization.

7.5 Project Closure

The project closing is the last process of all project processes and the most often neglected one. Project closure is more than packing things up and starting to move right into planning the next project. The closing process consists of two sub-processes: Contract closeout and administrative closure.

The contract closeout process is performed and completed before the administrative closure process begins. Both processes are concerned with verifying that the work of the project was completed correctly and to the stakeholders' satisfaction. One of the most important functions of this process is obtaining formal acceptance of the product of the project from stakeholders and customers. The goal of closing is to get an official sign-off from the stakeholders acknowledging acceptance of the product and to file this with the project documents.

After delivering a successful project to the customers and stakeholders the project must come to end. For this, a successful end has to be defined. Delivering only the product or service of the project doesn't mean it's been completed satisfactorily. It has to meet or exceed the stakeholders' expectations.
These expectations and the project end are reached by documenting the acceptance of the product of the project with a formal sign-off and filing it with records for the future reference during the closing process.

7.5.1 Characteristics of Closing

A few general characteristics concern all projects during the closing process. During the closing, the probability of completing the project is at its highest and the risk is at its lowest.

The major part of the work of the project is done and so the probability of completing is very high. Furthermore, the probability of not finishing the project is very low if not all of the work is completed during this process.

There are several different reasons why projects can come to an end. In the best case the project has been completed successfully instead of being cancelled or killed before completion.

A "**normal**" completed project is simply the most common circumstance for project closure. The finish of a project, such as building a new facility, is marked by the transfer of ownership to the customer. In other projects, the end can be marked by handing out the final design to the production department, the creation of a new product or the output is incorporated into ongoing operations.

"**Premature**" project closure describes the finishing of a project while some parts of the project have been eliminated. This can occur by the pressure put on the organization to finish a project or product because of, for example, the market situation. The risks and implications associated with this decision should be reviewed carefully and assessed by all stakeholders and the management.

Contrary to this, **perpetual** project closing describes the circumstance in which some projects develop a life of their own because they never seem to end. This phenomenon is not only caused by delays. Often the major characteristic is constant add-ons to the project.
The customer continuously requires small changes that will improve the project outcome. These changes represent add-ons perceived as being part of the original project intent like adding features to software or to product design. The constant add-ons are typically to indicate poor definition of the project scope but the phenomenon can be reduced by the clear definition of project scope and limitations.

Audit groups or project managers have several alternatives available for projects displaying characteristics of becoming perpetual. They can limit resources, budget or time and redefine the project end or scope to force the closure.

These alternatives should be designed to bring the project to an end as quickly as possible in order to limit additional costs and gain the positive benefits of a completed project.

Of course, some projects simply fail but this circumstance is rarer. In practice, it is possible that the planned project is not realizable. Developing a prototype of a new product or technology can show that the original concept will be unworkable. Another example can be the developing of a new pharmaceutical drug. The project may need to be canceled because of unsustainable side effects.

The reflection of changes in organizational direction is important to the project team because this change can have a big effect. Normally the changes are small over a long period of time but sometimes major shifts in an organization require dramatic shifts in priority. In this change period, projects in process may need to be modified or cancelled. A project can start with a high priority but maybe crash during its project life cycle as conditions change.

7.5.2 Contract Closeout

The Contract closeout process is concerned with completing and settling the terms of the contract. It also determines if the work described in the contract was completed accurately and satisfactorily. This process is called product verification. The product verification performed during the closing process determines if all of the work of the project was completed correctly and satisfactorily according to stakeholder expectations.

Contract closeout also updates records and archives the information for future reference. These records detail the final results of the work of the project. Sometimes contracts have specific conditions or terms for completion and closeout. These terms or conditions should be made known to all parties involved so that project closure isn't postponed because of missing an important detail. The project team has to know if there are any special terms so as to prevent an accidental delay in the contract or project closure.

The contract closeout has one input and one tool and technique. The input to this process is contract documentation. This includes the contract itself and all the supporting documents that belong to the contract. These attachments could be documents like the work breakdown structure, the project schedule, change control documents, technical documents, financial and payment records and quality control inspection results. All information gathered during the project are filed once the project is closed out so that anyone considering a future project of similar scope can reference what was already done.

One of the purposes of the contract closeout process is to provide formal notice to the seller, usually in written form, that the contract is complete. The project manager has to document the formal acceptance of the contract. Often the provisions for formalizing acceptance of the product and closing the contract are spelled out in the contract itself.

If an extra procurement department exists which handles the contract administration, that department will be expected to inform the project management when the contract is completed and will in turn follow the formal procedures to let the seller know the contract is complete. The contract completion should then be noted in the copy of the project records.

This process is the organizational way of formally accepting the product of the project from the vendor and closing out the contract. If the product or service does not meet expectations, the vendor will need to correct any problems before a formal acceptance notice is issued.
Normally quality audits are performed during the course of the project and the vendor is given the opportunity to make corrections earlier in the process than at the closing stage. To avoid any problem, it is wrong to wait until the very end of the project and then spring all the problems and issues on the vendor at that time. It's much more efficient to discuss each problem with a vendor as it appears as this provides the vendor with the opportunity to correct them as and when they occur.

Formal acceptance and closure is one of the outputs of the contract closeout process. The other output is called the contract file. This is simply all the contract records and supporting documents.

These records are indexed for easy reference and included as inputs to the administrative closure process. Then, at the conclusion of administrative closure, project archives, which include the contract records, are filed for future reference.

7.5.3   Administrative Closure

The key activity of the administrative closure process is concerned with gathering and disseminating information to formalize project closure. Every project requires closure and the completion of each project phase requires administrative closure as well. Administrative closure shouldn't wait until project completion but rather should be performed at the end of every phase.

Administrative closure verifies and documents the project outcomes just like the contract closeout process. It is important to know that not all projects are performed under contract but all projects require an administrative closure.

Since verification and documentation of the project outcomes occur in both processes, projects that are performed under contract need to have project results verified only once. When the project outcomes are documented, formal acceptance is requested of the stakeholders.

The Administrative closure process gathers all the project records and verifies that they are up to date and accurate. The project records must correctly identify the final specifications of the product or service the project sent out to produce. Administrative closure is in place to ensure this information accurately reflects the true results of the project.

The three inputs to this process are **performance measurement documents, product documentation** and **other records which are related to the project**.

All of the **performance measurements** that were used to analyze project progress during the controlling processes are included as part of the documentation for the administrative closure process.

Any document that helped establish the basis for the performance measurements, like the project plan, the cost budget, cost estimates and the project schedule are also collected here. Finally, these documents are reviewed to make certain the goals and objectives of the project were met successfully.

Each of these documents should be available for review during the administrative closure process. According to the formal acceptance of the project by the stakeholders, the executive management team or the customer may request to see this documents.

The second input of administrative closure is **product documentation**. This documentation includes anything that details the product or service of the project. This details things like the requirements documents, specifications, plans, technical documents, electronic files and drawings. The input includes all information that details or lists the product specifications or requirements. Also these documents should be available for review such as the performance documents.

Of course, it is possible that projects work very well and without any problems: he projects just falls into place according to the plan, the team functions at the performance stage and the customers and stakeholders are happy. It will be difficult to close these projects because they have progressed particularly well and still work. The majority of projects can fall into this category if the team practice good project management techniques and exercise those great communication skills.

At the end, the last outputs of the last process of your project will be the project

- archives,
- project closure & formal acceptance and
- lessons learned.

Project Archives: When all the work of the project is completed, the vendor is paid, the contract is closed, and the records are gathered and project archives will be created. These include any project documents completed during the project.

All of the inputs to this process are included here as well as the contract documents. Keep in mind that if projects are performed under contract, the archiving of financial records is especially important. These records may need to be accessed if there are payment disputes. Furthermore, this information is especially useful when estimating future projects. Projects with large financial expenditures also require particular attention to the archiving of financial records for the same reasons.

All of these documents should indexed for reference and filed in a safe place. They will include electronic databases and electronic documents as part of the project archives as well. These records can be stored on a network drive or copied onto a CD that's kept with the project binder. The organizational policies will dictate how the project records should be filed. If no policies exist, they have to be created.

Project Closure and Formal Acceptance: The project closure output concerns verifying that the product of the project meets all requirements and obtains formal sign-off of the acceptance of the product. Formal acceptance also includes distributing notice of the acceptance of the product or service of the project by the stakeholders and customers. Documenting formal acceptance is important because it signals the official closure of the project and it confirms that the project was completed satisfactorily. In this form, a document for sign-off indicates that the signing person accepts the product of the project.

Another important function of sign-off is that it signifies the beginning of the warranty period. The warranty of work for a time period after completing a project is often used in projects that produce software programs. Typically, in the case of software projects, bugs are fixed for free during the warranty period. In this case, the critical point is that the warranty that has to indicate exactly what is covered.

Lessons Learned: The purpose of lessons learned is the same as the processes before but they document the successes and failures of the project, too. As an example, lessons learned documents the reasons why specific corrective actions were taken, unplanned risks that occurred, mistakes that were made and could have been avoided.

There are facts that can be learned from failed projects as well as successful projects and this information, whether good or bad, should be documented for future reference. Often this work is not done because a lot of employees don't want to admit to making mistakes or learning from mistakes made during the project. It could be disagreeable to associate their name with failed projects or even mistakes.

Organizations that do not document lessons learned probably do conduct post-implementation audits. Documenting and gathering information during this procedure can serve the same function as lessons learned if they include the good and the bad alike. Post-implementation audits aren't an official output, but they go hand in hand with lessons learned as they examine the project from beginning to end and look at what went right and what went wrong.

At the conclusion of the project the team members will be released and return to their functional managers or new projects. This release is a non-official process but it should be noted at the end of the project. When the project is getting closer to completion the managers should be informed what the schedule looks like so that they can start planning activities and scheduling activity dates.

7.6 Project Closure

This chapter illustrated the necessity of different aspects of preparing and executing parts of the project management process. Starting with a good preparation is a must. Good documentation is an essential basic for all further steps in the management process. The audits are performed to ascertain the validity and reliability of information, and also to provide an assessment of a system's internal control. It gives any organization the chance to prove its excellence and therefore the chance to generate profits e.g. by getting a big contract with a new customer.

The termination and closure process shows the significance of ending a project efficiently and under cost control aspects. Also, the learning benefits, even from a terminated project, may help to improve further projects. Project closure is the most often neglected process of all the project management processes.

The closure can be defined by four important aspects, which are:

- Checking the work for completeness and accuracy.
- Documenting formal acceptance.
- Disseminating project closure information.
- Archiving records and lessons learned.

The two processes in the closing group are contract closeout and administrative closure. Contract closeout is performed before administrative closure and is concerned with settling the contract and completing the contract according to its terms. Its two outputs are contract file and formal acceptance and closure.

Administrative closure is performed at the end of each phase of the project as well as at the end of the project. Administrative closure involves documenting formal acceptance and disseminating notice of acceptance to the stakeholders, customer and others. All documentation gathered during the project and collected during this process is archived and saved for reference purposes on future projects.

Lessons learned documents the successes and failures of the project. Many times lessons learned are not documented because staff members do not want to assign their names to project errors or failures. Documenting these "learned from past" experiences can avoid the repetition of the same errors in new projects.

8 Final Remarks and further Readings

I hope this book provided you with some helpful tools and examples with which to achieve faster and better results in your project work. There are certain different approaches as to how to best handle project management and the approach used in this book is based upon my experiences, which may vary from the experience of other project managers. However, there is one point on which all experts will come to the same conclusion: When you are undertaking project management, do it professionally and be always willing to accept the knowledge gained from the project experience of other people. As shown in this book, project managements cover so many areas of expertise that rarely can any one person be found who is the master of all of them.

Also, certain topics which I also regard as quite important could only be touched upon in this book, e.g. project management software or management approaches to project management. If you are interested in learning more about project management, I have found the following books extremely helpful as they cover a broad range of project management experiences and manage to bridge the gap between practical approaches and theoretical knowledge. I have also used some of these approaches in designing my lectures and therefore they have also been of great use when putting together this book:

Duncan, W.R.: A Guide to the Project Management Body of Knowledge, Project Management Institute, Upper Darby; 1996.

Gray, Clifford F. and Erik W. Larson: Project Management – The managerial process; 4th edition; New York, 2008.

Johansson, Henry J. et.al.: Business Process Reengineering: BreakPoint Strategies for Market Dominance; John Wiley & Sons; 1993.

and last but not least the homepage of the Project Management Institute www.pmi.org.

9 Endnotes

1. The Activity-On-Arrow (AOA) method uses arrows to represent activities and nodes represent events. A great advantage of AOA is the simple drawing and the easy understanding of the network diagram. Path tracing is simplified by event numbering scheme. The activity-on-arrow diagram doesn't need a network or complete information to show activity sequence and dependencies. Additional milestones and events can be flagged easily. The activity-on-arrow approach needs dummy activities to clarify dependency relationships and give each of them its unique identification number.
2. www.tensteppb.com
3. McMinn, Robert D.: The Project Life Cycle: The Termination Phase, 2000.

www.ingramcontent.com/pod-product-compliance
Lightning Source LLC
Chambersburg PA
CBHW050111230526
45470CB00004B/1787